MW00977052

PRAISE GOETH BEFORE THEE

PRAISE GOETH BEFORE THEE

▼

A Study of the Praise Life of the Believer

Kenneth W. Jones

Writer's Showcase
New York Lincoln Shanghai

Praise Goeth Before Thee
A Study of the Praise Life of the Believer

All Rights Reserved © 2002 by Kenneth W. Jones

No part of this book may be reproduced or transmitted in any form or by any means, graphic, electronic, or mechanical, including photocopying, recording, taping, or by any information storage retrieval system, without the written permission of the publisher.

Writer's Showcase
an imprint of iUniverse, Inc.

For information address:
iUniverse
2021 Pine Lake Road, Suite 100
Lincoln, NE 68512
www.iuniverse.com

Copyrights as a ministry of Practical Living Ministry, June, 2001

ISBN: 0-595-25954-5 (Pbk)
ISBN: 0-595-65461-4 (Cloth)

Printed in the United States of America

CONTENTS

Exhorted To Praise 1

Introduction 7

Chapter One, Praise As A Weapon In Battle 11

Chapter Two, The Advantages Of Praise To The Believer 21

Chapter Three, The Story Of Jehoshaphat 29
    SEND JUDAH FIRST! 32

Chapter Four, The Names For Praise 37
    NAMES FOR PRAISE 38

Chapter Five, Worship Sustaineth Thee 45

Chapter Six, Our First Ministry 53
    RESULTS OF WORSHIP: 54

Chapter Seven, God's Prescribed Order 59
    DOING ALL THINGS WELL 64
    Nadab and Abihu 67
    Is God Glorified? 70
    Keeping the Flesh out of our Worship 71

Moses and the Rock 72
Doing it the way He commanded 75

Chapter Eight, Victory In Praise 81

Chapter Nine, Praise And The Anointing 87
How is the Anointing Released? 88
We Increase in the Anointing by Desiring God's Presence 89
Why Do We Need the Anointing in Our Lives? 90

Final Encouragement 93

PRAISE GOETH BEFORE THEE

Exhorted To Praise

Psalms 149:1-9

1   Praise the LORD. Sing to the LORD a new song, his praise in the assembly of the saints.

2   Let Israel rejoice in their Maker; let the people of Zion be glad in their King.

3   Let them praise his name with dancing and make music to him with tambourine and harp.

4   For the LORD takes delight in his people; he crowns the humble with salvation.

5   Let the saints rejoice in this honor and sing for joy on their beds.

6   May the praise of God be in their mouths and a double-edged sword in their hands,

7   to inflict vengeance on the nations and punishment on the peoples,

8   to bind their kings with fetters, their nobles with shackles of iron,

9   to carry out the sentence written against them. This is the glory of all his saints. Praise the LORD. (NIV)

As believers, we are encouraged, directed, and required to Praise the Lord. David in the last five chapters of Psalms reminds Israel over and over again to praise the Lord. The last four chapters of Psalms begin with

"Praise the Lord!" So it is obvious that it is vital for believers to render praise, worship, and adoration to the King of Kings and Lord of Lords.

David was a man of praise. He rejoiced consistently before the Lord of his salvation. He praised the Father with such affection as one who realized the awesomeness of God's power, and His glory. He praised as one who understood God's mercy, goodness and His strength available to all that call upon Him with a sincere heart.

Psalms 40:2-3:

2   *He brought me up also out of an horrible pit, out of the miry clay, and set my feet upon a rock, and established my goings.*

3   *And he hath put a new song in my mouth, even praise unto our God: many shall see it, and fear, and shall trust in the LORD.*

David had found himself in a *"horrible pit"*—a place of destruction and desolation in which there was no hope. He was on miry clay, meaning *the ground had no substance in order to sustain or support him.* God picked him up out of that mess, set his feet upon a rock, and steadied his steps. ***God gave him a cause to rejoice and now David's mouth was filled with a new song, giving praise to God.*** Through this renewed hope, a new song was placed in David's heart and a life of praise was established.

In the last few chapters of Psalms, he avowed that he would bless God with grateful and affectionate praise. Every day with new reasons, he would bless the Lord. He considered praise appropriate for those who are upright and love the Lord (Psalms 33:1). He did not hesitate to use instruments of music to rejoice in the God of his salvation. History records him *dancing before the Lord with all his might as one who was beside himself* (**2 Samuel 6:14**). He dedicated himself to praise while he had breath in his body and while he had being (still alive) (Psalms 104:33).

Here in **Psalms 149**, David calls upon Israel to sing unto the Lord a new song and to praise Him in the assembly of the saints. In verse 3, he declares that God's name will be praised in the choir and in the dance and with the tambourine and lyre. *Let the saints be joyful in the glory and beauty of God and let them sing for joy upon their beds!* This is the type of praise that should be in our churches today. There should be exuberant praise and intimate worship among the saints who glory in their Lord. God created us for fellowship and to demonstrate His praises in the earth. When saints praise the Father, the whole world comes to know of the power and glory of our God. God, Himself, delights in us and joins in our celebration.

Zeph 3:17 "The LORD your God is in your midst, a victorious warrior. He will exult over you with joy, He will be quiet in His love, He will rejoice over you with shouts of joy." (NAS)

When God comes down, His presence revives, strengthens, and blesses us. He is able to fight for you, restore you, as He rejoices in your presence. Praise is not for some egotistical God who needs to be built up. Praise opens a portal, a gateway, by which God can meet with His people and bless them. His presence provides direction, comfort, refreshment, joy and strength. **Psalms 16:11** says, *"In His presence is fullness of joy and the pleasures of life forevermore."* **Colossians 2:3** says, *"In whom are hidden all the treasures of wisdom and knowledge."* All these things are available to you as you enter into His presence with praise and worship.

Isaiah 43:21: *"This people have I formed for myself; they shall shew forth my praise."*

This people have I formed for myself. God formed us, created us for a special purpose. His purpose is to preserve the remembrance of His name, to transmit the knowledge of the true God through all generations, and to celebrate His praise in all the earth. It is therefore our duty to show forth or demonstrate His praise, not only with our lips, but also in our lives, by giving ourselves to His service.

They shall show forth (demonstrate) my praise. They shall celebrate His goodness and shall reveal that they are His people. No one buys any major article or product today without a good demonstration to see if it works. When we show the world that we are delighted in our God and it is demonstrated through our praise, they too, will hunger for God and seek after Him. However, if we walk around grumbling, faultfinding, and defeated, we will not find too many people who would desire what we say we have.

Psalms is the largest book of the bible. It means in Hebrew, "Praise Songs." In the Greek, *Psalmoi,* means *"songs to the accompaniment of stringed instruments."* Psalms is divided into 5 books, or divisions. The first three divisions of Psalms always end in "Amen." The writers were more concerned about their prayers unto God and He hearing their cry for help and deliverance. The fourth division of Psalms (Psalms 106) ends with Hallelujah and Amen as it remembers the goodness and works of God. The final division ends with Hallelujah! The last six chapters of Psalms are wholly taken up in praising God. There is not one word of complaint or petition in them. This represents that as we come closer to God, being made more in the image of Christ, we should be full of the praises of God. Our prayers should evolve into praises as we remember the goodness and faithfulness of our God.

I exhort you to praise today. As you read this book, open your heart to God and then your mouth to sing out songs of deliverance, power, and praise to the Almighty God. There is one thing we do here on earth that we will continue to do in heaven. That is to praise and worship God. That is why we should view our life here on earth as choir practice for heaven. To say that worship and praise is the most important aspect of ministry today is an understatement. In light of this, there is no more important activity of the spirit, soul, and body of man than to praise and worship.

We are practicing here on earth what the heavenly host is doing in heaven around the throne of God right now (**Revelation 19:1**). Prayers will one day be swallowed up in everlasting praises to our loving Father. *This is the destiny of the believer who praises God with his whole heart.*

PRAISE GOETH BEFORE THEE

INTRODUCTION

No religion or practice of faith is exempt or without the exercise or exhibition of praise and worship to some creator or being. Webster's Dictionary defines praise as the extolling of a deity, ruler, or hero; an expression of approval or admiration. Webster further defines worship as a reverent love and allegiance accorded a deity, idol, or sacred object. Both praise and worship describes an action that is directed towards something or someone. In the Christian faith, God is the object of our affection and admiration. The bible teaches that God ordained and decreed that His creation should praise and worship His name in response to His mighty acts and benevolence to humanity.

Before the foundations of the world, God created an angelic host who remains encamped around His throne, and will forever be throughout eternity to praise and worship His name (Revelation 5:11.12). God even created Lucifer, an anointed Cherub, specifically for praise. He placed instruments of praise inside his body and directed him to lead the angelic host in worship until iniquity was found in him (Ezekiel 28:14). Out of love, God created man for fellowship. God then formed a people for Himself (Isaiah 43:21) to demonstrate or show forth His praise in the earth. All of this leads me to one conclusion that God desires praise and worship and that praise is an integral part of our relationship with God. It is the foundation of our faith and demonstration of our allegiance to the one who created us and provides us with good things.

Then why does it appear that I am serving some egotistical God who demands my reverence, respect, and homage? It is a mystery that as I direct my praise and affection to God that I, in turn, am renewed, refreshed, and my faith strengthened. This causes me to think that praise and worship is not just directed to God, but that it gives me an opportunity to open a "line of communication," by which God can minister unto me.

David said in Psalms 33:1 that *Praise is comely for the upright.* Further translation clarifies this statement by saying that praise is fitting, appropriate, and becoming of the upright in heart. I worship God because it is my nature to worship and praise Him. I am a praise being, created for fellowship and destined to praise a loving, caring, powerful, God. There are several reasons why believers should praise God:

(1) We praise God because God is Good. We serve a good God who does good things.

> *"For the LORD is good; his mercy is everlasting; and his truth endureth to all generations." (Psalms 100:5)*

(2) Because God made us and given us all things to enjoy.

> *"The heavens declare his righteousness, and all the people see his glory." (Psalms 97:6)*

We are God's creation, created by His handiwork, to offer up spiritual sacrifices of praise unto His name (1 Peter 2:5). We praise Him in response to the many blessings He has provided for us.

> *"According as his divine power hath given unto us all things that pertain unto life and godliness, through the knowledge of him that hath called us to glory and virtue:" (2 Peter 1:3)*

Now there are times when I say, "I haven't been feeling blessed lately." Well, God has provided the blessings, but I must incorporate them by faith. But that is another subject. It is as I focus on God's blessings that praise is generated in my heart causing me to respond with thanksgiving and rejoicing.

(3) We praise God because of the stability of His counsel or purposes for our lives.

> *"He layeth up sound wisdom for the righteous: he is a buckler to them that walk uprightly. He keepeth the paths of judgment, and preserveth the way of his saints." (Proverbs 2:7-8)*

I have come to appreciate those individuals in my life who have provided me with insight, wisdom, guidance, and purpose. The same should be for all believers who walk in the counsel of the Lord. God preserves or guides the way of His children to keep them from falling into the snares of life.

(4) Most importantly, we praise God in response to the blessings that He bestows upon those who acknowledge Him to be their God— blessings of care, protection, and deliverance in danger.

> *"He that dwelleth in the secret place of the most High shall abide under the shadow of the Almighty. I will say of the LORD, He is my refuge and my fortress: my God; in him will I trust. Surely he shall deliver thee from the snare of the fowler, and from the noisome pestilence." (Psalms 91:1-3)*

The whole 91st chapter of Psalms is dedicated to praising God for His protection, blessings, direction, wisdom, and power. As children of God, we sing praises unto Him who is our provider, shelter, strong tower, all-sufficient one, our righteousness, and our strength. Praise is a way of life for the child of God, who was created by God, and for God, to enjoy all the blessings that He has provided for us.

The purpose of this book is to help you understand the importance of praise and worship in the life of the believer. As you read this book, I pray that you come into a deeper, clearer, understanding of what God desires to accomplish in His children through the avenue of praise. I invite you to take every opportunity to stand before Him and render to Him the praise that is due His marvelous name. Let everything that has breath, praise the Lord! (Psalms 150:6) Amen.

▼

CHAPTER ONE

PRAISE AS A WEAPON IN BATTLE

For years, the concept of praise was foreign to me. I mean, I would sing songs in church and listen to others sing, but to me, it was more of a ritual. Then as I came to know the Lord personally, and intimately, praise became more meaningful and enjoyable. Then one day I learned through the scriptures that God intended for me to use praise as a weapon in spiritual battle. The idea of employing praise to defeat some spiritual being was even more far fetched in the beginning. However, after intense study of the scriptures, it became apparent to me that praise can be the most powerful asset available to the believer in his battle against the spiritual forces that would seek to destroy him and hinder his or her walk with God.

In case you didn't know, we are involved in a spiritual battle, against spiritual forces, and to be even more precise, against the devil.

> *Finally, my brethren, be strong in the Lord, and in the power of his might. Put on the whole armour of God, that ye may be able to stand against the wiles of the devil. For we wrestle not against*

flesh and blood, but against principalities, against powers, against the rulers of the darkness of this world, against spiritual wickedness in high places. (Ephesians 6:10-12)

When I was saved, I was enlisted into God's Army and deployed onto a spiritual battleground to take on the devil. God gave me special armor (Ephesians 6: 13-17) to be able to stand against the wiles of the devil. However, the word, "stand" used here in the Greek means to be able *to hold on, or hold your ground.* It's good to be able to hold on and hold your ground, but I want a weapon to destroy the works of the devil. I wanted to take him out. In the military, when we come under a ground attack, our first mission is to take out the enemy's main gun. When I am under Satan's attack, I will stand in faith, but I want to knock out the main source of his power so that I can put an end to his onslaught.

Thanks be to God for giving me the spiritual weapons to handle any attack that Satan launches against me. He's given me protection such as the breastplate of righteousness to protect my heart and my inner man. He's given me the helmet of salvation to guard my thoughts and help me cast down wicked imaginations. I have my loins girded around me with the truth of God's Word that is able to hold me up in the midst of adversity. My feet are shod with the preparation of the gospel of peace, as others can be a witness to my victory and come to receive Christ.

God has also given me offensive weapons by which to fight with. With the "Sword of the Spirit," I am able to slash through the enemy defenses and expose his plots. With the "shield of faith," I am to repel his fiery darts, and push him back. Yet, I need more power in order to destroy the works of Satan or at least render the devil "combat ineffective" in my life. To destroy Satan's works means to destroy his plans of wickedness, and his control over my life. God has given me that power through praise. David taught me this lesson by showing me how the Israelites employed praise as part of their battle strategy.

Ps 149:6-9 {Let} the high praises of God {be} in their mouth, and a two-edged sword in their hand,

7   *To execute vengeance on the nations, and punishment on the peoples;*

8   *To bind their kings with chains, and their nobles with fetters of iron;*

9   *To execute on them the judgment written; this is an honor for all His godly ones. Praise the LORD! (NAV)*

Praise in the life of David was also a strategy, or one may say, a weapon in battle. All armies train with marching drills involving some type of chant or song in the conduct of its movement. *"Let the high praises of God be in their mouth,"* in Hebrew, literally means, *"Praises of God in their throat; and a sword of two edges in their hand."* That is, in the very work of executing the purposes of God on his enemies, there should be the feeling and the language of praise. Our hearts should be full of confidence in God, being engaged in his service; and while we defend ourselves, or face the enemies of God, we should chant His praise.

David was encouraging the people of Israel to go out with praise and a two-edged sword in their hands. *That two edge-sword that cuts both ways is the Word of God (Hebrews 4:12). We use praise that flows from our tongue and the Word of God to slash through the enemy encampments and defenses, to inflict punishment upon his attacking hordes, and take back all he has stole from us. We also gain vengeance upon him for all the things he has put us through.* Wouldn't you like to get even with the devil for having you out there in the world, lost and without God, for destroying your loved ones, and robbing you of your health, joy, finances, and peace? Then take the Word of God and begin to shout the Praises of God and go on the offense today and put that devil to flight!

Matthew 16:18: "And I say also unto thee, That thou art Peter, and upon this rock I will build my church; and the gates of hell shall not prevail against it." (KJV)

Many times we read this scripture and think that the church is on the defense, trying to hold back the devil and his forces. On the contrary, we are on the Offense! The word, "prevail," in the Greek means to *"overcome or overpower."* Praise (especially, when you sing the Word of God), puts you on the offense and the gates of Hell will not be able to hold you back from getting all that God has for you. They will not be able to overcome you or keep you from doing what God called you to do. That is Good News!

David goes on in verse 8 of Psalms 149, ***"To bind their kings with chains and their nobles with fetters of iron."*** *That means to render them ineffective and take them prisoner.* Jesus talks about the power of binding and loosing. We have that power as believers to take the enemy captive. At the end of a battle, the defeated general would be marched in a parade before the people as they cheered with victory. *Praise, in line with the Word of God, renders the enemy ineffective and you become a witness of his defeat.* I hate it when people say, "Give the devil his due," as in recognizing that Satan is at work in the lives of people and doing a good job at it. Well, the due that is to be paid to the devil is the lake of fire that burns with fire and brimstone (**Rev 20:10**). We can generate some heat for him today by praising the Lord and putting him to flight each time he rears his ugly head.

So what am I saying to you? The key to victorious Christian living is to understand the necessity, the importance, and the power of praise. God has given you a powerful weapon by which you can put the enemy to flight and render his attacks against you useless and without power.

Ps 8:2 Out of the mouth of babes and sucklings hast thou ordained strength because of thine enemies, that thou mightest still the enemy and the avenger.

The word, *"strength,"* used here in the Hebrew means *"praise."* It also means, *"power."* So praise, strength, and power are associated together. In other words, *there is power in praise; there is strength in praise.* The psalmist, David knew the importance of praise. He was considered to be a mighty warrior and he knew a lot about battle. So praise strengthened him with confidence in battle.

The word, *"still"* in the Hebrew means *to put down and away, to make to rest, to rid of, or to take away.* The word, "shabath" is the root word of "still" which means *to desist from exertion; to cease.* Further translation of **Psalms 8:2** reads *"Out of the mouths of children, God's children, has God established praise (and power) because of thine enemies, that we might put to rest, take away the power, still the operations of the enemy and the avenger."*

God gave us this power of praise *because of thine enemies.* God knew we would have to contend for the faith and that we would have to deal with an enemy. Therefore, He (God) provided us a weapon by which we can overcome the operations and devices of the evil one. In **Ephesians 6:10-12**, God says, *"Be strong in the Lord (be empowered through your union with Him); draw our strength from Him which His boundless might provides* (Amplified Version). *God releases His might through Praise.*

David would tend the sheep of his father, Jesse and would spend countless hours in praise to the Lord God of Israel. Praise strengthened him so that he was able to handle any creature, foe, or attack of the enemy.

1 Sam 17:34-37: And David said unto Saul, Thy servant kept his father's sheep, and there came a lion, and a bear, and took a lamb out of the flock: And I went out after him, and smote him, and delivered it out of his mouth: and when he arose against me, I caught him by his beard, and smote him, and slew him. Thy servant slew both the lion and the bear: and this uncircumcised Philistine shall be as one of them, seeing he hath defied the armies of the living God. David said moreover, The LORD that delivered me out of the paw of the lion, and out of the paw of the bear, he will deliver me out of the hand of this Philistine. And Saul said unto David, Go, and the LORD be with thee.

Notice that David never ran from the enemy, but always towards or after him. Praise builds faith that encourages the believer so that in the midst of trouble, he will not take flight, but stand and fight, armed with God's armor, His Word, and a song of victory in his heart. The word, *"encourage"* means *to inspire with hope; to give support to; and to inspire courage and confidence.* As we face trials, disappointments, persecutions, and moments of hopelessness, we need to praise the Father and be inspired with hope in the faithfulness of our God. As we face situations that seem to overwhelm us, praise will give us the courage to stand and the confidence that God will see us through. This doesn't mean that the enemy or trials will go away, but if we allow praise to go before thee, God enters the battle first to fight on our behalf.

> *"And all this assembly shall know that the LORD saveth not with sword and spear: for the battle is the LORD's, and he will give you into our hands." (1 Samuel 17:47) (KJV)*

> *"The LORD shall fight for you, and ye shall hold your peace." (Exodus 14:14)*

David did not run towards Goliath as a warrior, but as a priest. A priest is one who offers up sacrifices unto God in obedience and faith. David knew that his physical weapons were no match against Goliath's sword and spear. But he knew that Goliath was no match for his God! I can hear David singing the praises of God as he approached his enemy.

> *"I will call upon the LORD, who is worthy to be praised: so shall I be saved from mine enemies." (Psalms 18:3) (KJV)*
> *"He teacheth my hands to war, so that a bow of steel is broken by mine arms.*
> *Thou hast also given me the shield of thy salvation: and thy right*

hand hath holden me up, and thy gentleness hath made me great.
Thou hast enlarged my steps under me, that my feet did not slip.
I have pursued mine enemies, and overtaken them: neither did I
turn again till they were consumed.
I have wounded them that they were not able to rise: they are fall-
en under my feet.
For thou hast girded me with strength unto the battle: thou hast
subdued under me those that rose up against me." (Psalms 18:34-
39) (KJV)

As David allowed praise to go before him, the power of God was
brought on the scene. His faith was empowered once again to defeat his
enemy. It was the priest who slain Goliath, not the warrior! *"For the*
weapons of our warfare are not carnal, but mighty through God to the
pulling down of strong holds (2 Corinthians 10:4). Praise is a spiritual
weapon available to the believer to assist not only in his walk with God,
but to empower him to stand against the wiles and attacks of the enemy.

Even in his battle with Goliath, David ran towards the enemy in full
assurance that God would give him the victory. He had confidence that
the same God that delivered him out of the paw of the lion and the bear
will give him victory over this Philistine (whom he considered a dog!).
David was a lion killer—a giant killer. **1ˢᵗ Peter 5:8** says Satan walks
around *"as a roaring lion."* Through praise you can become a lion killer
and put the devil on the run when he sees you coming.

In **Psalms 8:2**, David relates the power of praise to his victory over
Goliath. Here you have a gigantic foe, defeated by *a child* or in one sense
of a word, *a suckling.* He credits his power over the enemy, Goliath, due to
his praise life with the Father. You may be facing a "Goliath" situation or
trial. *Through praise, you can bring that trial or circumstance down and gain*
the victory. Satan is defeated when we release praise from our lips. It
releases the power of God over that situation or circumstance facing us.

Another translation of Psalms 8:2 is *"Out of the mouths of babes and sucklings thou has perfected praise."* This is the source of God's strength in the believer. Praise strengthens us to stand in the midst of trials until our victory comes. The New International Version says it even better by stating God has *"ordained praise"*. To ordain *means to order, to institute, or to establish. God instituted praise and placed it in the church.* Praise is not an option, nor is it a suggestion, **it is a command from God**. Unfortunately, many Christians do not see it as such and require much appeal by song leaders in order for them to enter into praise. *God knows what you need in order to be victorious, so He made it mandatory that praise be of the utmost importance in your life.*

I remember as a worship leader I would get in front of people and sometimes they were a rough crowd. Some people would stand there with their arms folded, looking at me as if to say, "Make me praise God!' Whew! That is why God told Jeremiah, "Be not dismayed at their faces (Jeremiah 1:17)." These people fail to realize that their attitudes would hinder them from enjoying new altitudes with Christ in the heavens. It was their loss and the enemy's gain. Meaning each time a person disobeys God" Word (and His Word commands us to praise Him), he or she gives ground to Satan. God ordained Praise in you, so release it and obtain the victory that comes with it.

I am a Field Artilleryman in the U.S. Army. The purpose of the artillery is to fire explosive rounds (by rockets or cannons) indirectly at the enemy to suppress, neutralize, harass, or destroy him. More importantly, we are to render him combat ineffective. Through the use of artillery barrages (firing thousands or rounds of rockets and explosive shells), we deprive him of his will to fight and normally he takes cover to prevent himself from being destroyed in the onslaught. That is what praise does to devil. The minute he begins his march, we should let go with praise to render him combat ineffective in our lives. We suppress (which means keeping the enemy from raising his head up to see the battlefield) him daily by living a life of praise, walking in the joy of the Lord.

More importantly, don't stop praising! Just because you survived one attack, does not mean there will not be another. Have you ever watched a western movie? Remember if the Sheriff killed someone in a fight, he still had to worry about his son, or brother who would soon come to avenge his death. Praise stills the enemy, but it also will take care of the avenger too! Too many Christians today are quick to stop praising when they feel the problem is gone, but don't stop! Just as in any military operation, there is always a counterattack. That means that the enemy will launch another attack in order to gain back the advantage. So live a life of praise. The avenger may come to take revenge, but you will be ready and not only still the enemy, but the avenger as well.

Getting back to military tactics, before any battle begin, both opposing sides fire artillery in attempt to shake up and destroy as much of the opponent forces as possible. **Ephesians 6:16** says Satan throws and propels fiery darts at us such as blasphemous thoughts, unbelief, a sudden temptation to do wrong, or thoughts that wound and torment the soul. They may come suddenly, like rockets, or from an enemy in ambush. Just as artillery, praise should go before the battle to render the enemy combat ineffective, extinguishing the flaming darts of the wicked one and putting him to flight so you won't even have to fight as hard if you have to fight at all.

Finally, the most important element of any combat operation is to fire a preparation of fire on the enemy's position well before the attack begins. Without a proper preparation of the battlefield, the amount of casualties suffered (loss of men and equipment) in the upcoming battle will be greater. Yet, with good preparation, the chance of success will be greater.

Many ministries, and churches, set out to do great things for God, but because they do not prepare the battleground with prayer and praise, they usually end up disgruntled, discouraged, and defeated. Allow praise to go before you in every situation of your life and ministry. God will provide you direction and strength as you open up the heavens with your songs of praise and worship. He will empower you, guide, and fight for you when praise goeth before thee.

CHAPTER TWO

▼

THE ADVANTAGES OF PRAISE TO THE BELIEVER

Because of Christ's death as a sin offering, or through him, believers are to demonstrate conduct befitting redeemed ones. They are to give praise and thanksgiving to God with a willing and full heart. They are to live a life that is pleasing to God, by not being conformed to this world and presenting themselves as living sacrifices which is their reasonable service or worship (Romans 12:1). The Old Testament ordinances called only for dead sacrifices, but what good is a dead sacrifice to God other than atonement? Jesus became the final sacrifice, so there is no need for it anymore. Pleasing God can ultimately be reduced to three fundamental practices or attitudes—praise, obedience, and submission. By this, we are able to walk in righteous fellowship with the Lord.

Hebrews 13:15…Through Him, therefore, let us constantly and at all times offer up to God a sacrifice of praise, which is the fruit of our lips that thankfully acknowledge and confess and glorify His name. (Amplified Bible)

How does Praise benefit the believer? In the life of the believer, Praise accomplishes two major things:

PRAISE STIMULATES FAITH
PRAISE HELPS RENEWS THE MIND OF THE BELIEVER

In the book of Hebrews, the writer is calling us to constantly offer up the sacrifice of praise. Praise should be a continual act in the life of the believer. David said in Psalms 34:1, *"I WILL bless the Lord at all times: his praise shall continually be in my mouth."* Note the first two words, "I WILL." Praise must be a decision of not only the heart, but also the soul. Our inner man or spirit man desires to worship the Lord, but many times our minds get in the way. Praise must be an act of one's own volition that must be performed daily and not just a Sunday morning, church service sing-a-long.

Did you know that around the throne of God praise and worship is continually going on and has gone on forever? Therefore it has been established that God desires that we praise him continually. Does that mean we are to be singing all the time? Of course not, Praise is more than just singing, it is a way of life that is revealed in our lifestyle and our words that brings glory to God. David said that he would praise God constantly: to bless the Lord at all times, upon all occasions. He resolves to seek all opportunities for it, and to renew his praises upon every fresh occurrence flowing from his relationship with the Father. If we hope to spend our eternity praising God, it is fitting that we should spend as much time here on earth doing the same.

In the before mentioned passage of scripture we find out that praise is not only an act of the will, but it is a sacrifice to God. Praise requires and it is a sacrifice. It is not just a sacrifice of your time that you render unto God. You are to praise God when you feel like it and when you don't feel like it. However, praise *"is a sacrifice."* It is something offered up to God to maintain our relationship with Him. The sacrifices offered up by the Jews to God such as the peace offerings were a type of species of offerings that were designed not only to produce peace or friendship with God, but to preserve it. Offerings such as the peace offering, were a sign of thankful acknowledgment for favors received or as a means to continue in the friendship and favor of God. Praise is a means of maintaining our favor and delight with God. Through praise and worship we keep our focus on our relationship with the Father and allow Him to maintain His relationship with us.

As we talk about continual praise before the Father, am I advocating that we go around singing all day and never getting anything done. No, of course not. I'm talking about having a "Praise Attitude." Having a praise attitude is where we are ever cognizant of the hand of God in our lives and always in a state of thankfulness and thoughtfulness of His mercy, His grace, His ability, and His love for us. Philippians 4:6-8 says that we should be fretful for nothing, having no anxiety about anything, but in everything, by prayer and petition make our requests known unto God. It also says that our thinking should be on things worthy of praise and reverence. As we allow our thoughts to be consumed with the things of God, peace will settle our hearts and minds in Christ Jesus. Too many believers today are stressed, oppressed, depressed, and perplexed because the things of God do not dominate their thoughts and praise is not continuous in their lives. Maintain a Praise Attitude and let the Praise of God be continually in your mouths. Your mouth is the key for it produces the Words of Life and Power able to deliver you and keep you in your walk with the Lord.

Which brings me to my next subject: "the fruit of your lips. The phrase "fruit of the lips." is a Hebraism, meaning what the lips produce; that is, words. It is hard to have praise and worship without words. Hebrews 13:15 states that with the fruit of our lips, words are produced that acknowledge, confess, and glorify His name. Christianity is called the

"Great Confession," meaning we live and die by the words we say. Proverbs 18:21: *"Death and life are in the power of the tongue: and they that love it shall eat the fruit thereof."(KJV)* David says in Psalms 34:2 that his life, his soul will make boast in the Lord.

Romans 10:17 says, *"So then faith cometh by hearing, and hearing by the word of God."* (KJV) Hebrews 13:15 says that the fruit of our lips giving glory to Name. One translation means, 'the fruit of our lips, confessing unto His Name." So Praise stimulates Faith by giving us opportunity to confess the Word of God before Him which builds faith in our inner man, our spirit man, and our soul as we hear the Word of God being spoken through our lips. Praise is like that artillery launcher I was talking about earlier that launches and propels the Word of God with music and singing at the encampments of the enemy rendering him combat ineffective in our lives and at the same time, strengthening our position with the Father God! As we hear the Word of God spoken, our faith should increase.

This is why Paul encourages us in Ephesians 5:19,20: *"Speaking to yourselves in psalms and hymns and spiritual songs, singing and making melody in your heart to the Lord; Giving thanks always for all things unto God and the Father in the name of our Lord Jesus Christ;* (KJV). As we speak to ourselves, meaning our souls and our spirit man, singing and making melody in our hearts unto the Lord, we are encouraged by His mighty acts and His great love for us. Praise must be in our mouths and be released through our lips so that faith can be produced in our heart. Praise comforts us and empowers us to believe God's Word and His promises.

1 Samuel 30:6-8 "And David was greatly distressed; for the people spake of stoning him, because the soul of all the people was grieved, every man for his sons and for his daughters: but David encouraged himself in the LORD his God."

7   *And David said to Abiathar the priest, Ahimelech's son, I pray thee, bring me hither the ephod. And Abiathar brought thither the ephod to David.*

8   *And David inquired at the LORD, saying, Shall I pursue after this troop? shall I overtake them? And he answered him, Pursue: for thou shalt surely overtake them, and without fail recover all. (KJV)*

David, again, provides an excellent example to us today. In this chapter of Samuel, the Amalekites attacked David and his people. They attacked the city of Ziklag and burned it with fire (1 Samuel 30:1,2), taking away the women captive, including David's two wives. The Amalekites were descendents of Esau (who gave up his birthright to Jacob), constantly at war with the children of Israel. Since the days of Moses, God had instructed the Jews to destroy all of them, but they disobeyed and the Amalekites became a thorn in their side for many more years until the days of Hezekiah. The Amalekites were known for conducting raids upon Israel when they least expected, stealing their women and property and destroying their cities. The Amalekites are like Satan and his hordes. The enemy comes without warning to steal, kill, and to destroy (John 10:10). That is why we must always be "Prayed Up" and "Praised Up." Attacks will come, but we are to repel them with the sword of the spirit and the high praises of God in our mouths.

Now two types of people emerged from this attack. David's men were dispirited and began to weep until they had no more strength to weep. I was like that once. I was so distressed in my soul that I would lay on the couch for three days with no energy to rise up. The men then turned their attention on their circumstances and the man who was leading them. That also sounds familiar doesn't it. They began to shift the blame of their ills upon their leader. At this time, they were considering "stoning" David because of what had happened. Your true self is the self that rises up in the midst of adversity or calamity. It is easy to praise God when things are going your way, but how you respond when things go awry measures your true faith and trust in God.

David faced his calamity with calmness. He was greatly distressed over losing his two wives and regarding his men who were now considering stoning him. *BUT…* The most powerful thing about the conjunction, "but," is that it cancels out what was said before it. The bible said that David began to encourage himself in the Lord. He began to remind himself of the promises of God. I believe being a man of praise that he began to strengthen himself the only way he knew how: through praise to the Father. He began to sing Psalms 3 reminding him that God was a shield and buckler and a deliverer.

Psalms 3:1-3: "LORD, how are they increased that trouble me! many are they that rise up against me. Many there be which say of my soul, There is no help for him in God. Selah. But thou, O LORD, art a shield for me; my glory, and the lifter up of mine head."(KJV)
David began to be encouraged that: *"Many are the afflictions of the righteous: but the LORD delivereth him out of them all (Ps 34:19)." (KJV)*

As David began to encourage and strengthen himself through praise, he asked for the Ephod. The Ephod was a vestment that the priests wore when seeking or inquiring of the Lord. This is the same as worship. He then asked God for instruction and God told him to pursue the enemy and He would give him the victory and that without fail would recover all. That is good news! Had he stayed at the pity party with his men, nothing would have been accomplished. Praise stimulates faith by reminding the believer of the promises and the ability of God.

Praise also gives the believer an advantage because it helps to renew the mind of the person who is praising God with the Word of God.

Romans 12:2 "And be not conformed to this world: but be ye transformed by the renewing of your mind, that ye may prove what is that good, and acceptable, and perfect, will of God. (KJV)

We renew our minds by hearing the Word of God and allowing it to gain ascendance in our thought life over the thoughts of the devil (2Corinthians 10:5)

2 Corinthians 10:4-5 "The weapons we fight with are not the weapons of the world. On the contrary, they have divine power to demolish strongholds. We demolish arguments and every pretension that sets itself up against the knowledge of God, and we take captive every thought to make it obedient to Christ." (NIV)

We said earlier that Praise is a powerful weapon in battle against the enemy. The above verse says that we fight a spiritual battle that requires spiritual weapons to demolish the enemy's strongholds. I believe that this battle must be won in the spiritual before we see the physical manifestation at times. Here we see that there is a battle being fought on the battlefield of the mind. As we sing or speak the Word of God to our souls and our spirits, we release power to demolish the strongholds of thoughts brought by the enemy in an effort to defeat us and bring us down. Renewing the mind is essential to the success of the believer. That is why praise is so important so that we can achieve the victory in the spiritual and release the power of God so that victory is won here on earth.

Many believers can sing on autopilot. Praising the Lord while their minds are on all kinds of things: bills, the kids, their home, etc. For some, the praise service is battle of staying focused on God and casting down all sorts of imaginations. That is why in Psalms 103, David tells his soul, his mind, to bless the Lord. He knew he had to bring his mind under subjection to his spirit to get the job done. That is why we need a renewed mind to be more effective in our praise and worship to the Father.

Isaiah 29:13: "Wherefore the Lord said, Forasmuch as this people draw near me with their mouth, and with their lips do honour me, but have removed their heart far from me, and their fear toward me is taught by the precept of men:"(KJV)

The Amplified Bibles states, "Their fear and reverence for Me are a commandment of men that is learned by repetition without any thought as to the meaning."

Too much of our praise has become head knowledge and not heart-produced. Satan seeks to nullify the Word of God in our hearts through the traditions of men (Mark 7:13). If we allow ourselves to praise God with all our hearts, singing the Word of God, in the way prescribed by the Word of God, being directed by the Holy Spirit, we can reach new heights in God and our minds would be refreshed and renewed from the presence of the Lord.

CHAPTER THREE

▼

THE STORY OF JEHOSHAPHAT

2 Chronicles 20:1-4: It came to pass after this also, that the children of Moab, and the children of Ammon, and with them other beside the Ammonites, came against Jehoshaphat to battle. Then there came some that told Jehoshaphat, saying, There cometh a great multitude against thee from beyond the sea on this side Syria; and, behold, they be in Hazazon-tamar, which is Engedi. And Jehoshaphat feared, and set himself to seek the LORD, and proclaimed a fast throughout all Judah.
And Judah gathered themselves together, to ask help of the LORD: even out of all the cities of Judah they came to seek the LORD.

The story of Jehoshaphat is one of the best illustrations that demonstrates to us the power of praise and worship, and how we can achieve victory in the face of the enemy. Jehoshaphat, the son of Asa, became king of Judah. **2 Chronicles 17:4-12** says that *he sought the Lord and did not walk after the doings of Israel* (which represented the world at that time). The words, **"sought" or "seek"** in the Hebrew, specifically means to worship. So Jehoshaphat was a man who worshipped God. He taught all of Judah to seek the Lord, so it wasn't hard to get the whole nation to come together in one accord to seek the Lord when the enemy came. God had established the kingdom into Jehoshaphat's hand that all nations feared him. Yet, for some reason, the enemy still tried to attack. Living a life of praise and worship does not mean you will never be attacked, but prepares you for when the enemy comes.

He set himself to seek (worship) the Lord, and, in the first place, to make God his friend. Those that would seek the Lord so as to find him, and to find favor with Him, must set (commit) themselves to seek Him, and must do it with fixedness of thought, with sincerity of intention, and with the utmost vigor and resolution to continue seeking him. Remember, God is a rewarder of them that diligently seek Him, not casually inquire **(Hebrews 11:6).**

2 Chronicles 20:5-9: And Jehoshaphat stood in the congregation of Judah and Jerusalem, in the house of the LORD, before the new court,

6   *And said, O LORD God of our fathers, art not thou God in heaven? and rulest not thou over all the kingdoms of the heathen? and in thine hand is there not power and might, so that none is able to withstand thee?*

7   *Art not thou our God, who didst drive out the inhabitants of this land before thy people Israel, and gavest it to the seed of Abraham thy friend for ever?*

8   *And they dwelt therein, and have built thee a sanctuary therein for thy name, saying,*

9   *If, when evil cometh upon us, as the sword, judgment, or pestilence, or famine, we stand before this house, and in thy presence, (for thy name is in this house,) and cry unto thee in our affliction, then thou wilt hear and help.*

PRAISE is an act of worship or acknowledgment by which the virtues or deeds of another are recognized and extolled. It also means to bless or to commend someone (in this case, the Lord) for the works that He has done. Jehoshaphat began to commend and bless God (in a way, to flatter Him) in verses 6 and 7, extolling the majesty and greatness of God. Then he reminds the Lord of His promise to His people. As we praise the Father, we thank Him and commend Him for His mighty acts and remind Him of His covenant with us to deliver, save, strengthen, bless, anoint, empower, and protect us. God is now reminded and must respond to His Word. He will always honor His Word.

And all Judah stood before the LORD, with their little ones, their wives, and their children. Then upon Jahaziel the son of Zechariah, the son of Benaiah, the son of Jeiel, the son of Mattaniah, a Levite of the sons of Asaph, came the Spirit of the LORD in the midst of the congregation; And he said, Hearken ye, all Judah, and ye inhabitants of Jerusalem, and thou king Jehoshaphat, <u>Thus saith the LORD unto you, Be not afraid nor dismayed by reason of this great multitude; for the battle is not yours, but God's</u>. To morrow go ye down against them: behold, they come up by the cliff of Ziz; and ye shall find them at the end of the brook, before the wilderness of Jeruel. Ye shall not need to fight in this battle: set yourselves, stand ye still, and see the salvation of the LORD with you, O Judah and Jerusalem: fear not, nor be dismayed; to morrow go out against them: for the LORD will be with you. And Jehoshaphat bowed his head with his face to the ground: and all Judah and the inhabitants of Jerusalem fell before the LORD, worshipping the LORD. And the Levites, of the children of the Kohathites, and of the children of the Korhites, stood up to praise the LORD God of Israel with a loud voice on high. (2 Chronicles 20:13-19)

This must have been quite a scene to behold! Their diligence to seek the Lord and bless His Name brought down the presence of God Himself to speak to His people, to inspire them to confidence and hope and to

Honor His covenant by fighting on their behalf. When we bring God on the scene through praise, the victory is ours. God then puts us in a position to see the enemy's defeat and see His power displayed before us. The whole kingdom responded to God's Word, by continuing to worship the Lord, standing up to praise Him with a loud voice.

Praise is our response to the hand of our God moving in our lives. It's hard to imagine anyone who has been touched by the Father, not praising Him for the things He has done. I know that there are some that say, "But you do not need to do all that shouting and dancing, getting all excited." Then tear it out of the bible! They stood up (which means they were on their feet), to praise the Lord with a loud voice on high (shouting and celebration went on)!

SEND JUDAH FIRST!

20-23 And they rose early in the morning, and went forth into the wilderness of Tekoa: and as they went forth, Jehoshaphat stood and said, Hear me, O Judah, and ye inhabitants of Jerusalem; Believe in the LORD your God, so shall ye be established; believe his prophets, so shall ye prosper. <u>And when he had consulted with the people, he appointed singers unto the LORD, and that should praise the beauty of holiness, as they went out before the army, and to say, Praise the LORD; for his mercy endureth for ever. And when they began to sing and to praise, the LORD set ambushments against the children of Ammon, Moab, and mount Seir, which were come against Judah; and they were smitten.</u> For the children of Ammon and Moab stood up against the inhabitants of mount Seir, utterly to slay and destroy them: and when they had made an end of the inhabitants of Seir, every one helped to destroy another.
24-29 And when Judah came toward the watch tower in the wilderness, they looked unto the multitude, and, behold, they were dead bodies fallen to the earth, and none escaped. And when Jehoshaphat and his people

came to take away the spoil of them, they found among them in abundance both riches with the dead bodies, and precious jewels, which they stripped off for themselves, more than they could carry away: and they were three days in gathering of the spoil, it was so much. And on the fourth day they assembled themselves in the valley of Berachah; for there they blessed the LORD: therefore the name of the same place was called, The valley of Berachah, unto this day. Then they returned, every man of Judah and Jerusalem, and Jehoshaphat in the forefront of them, to go again to Jerusalem with joy; for the LORD had made them to rejoice over their ene-mies. And they came to Jerusalem with psalteries and harps and trumpets unto the house of the LORD. And the fear of God was on all the kingdoms of those countries, when they had heard that the LORD fought against the enemies of Israel.

The next day, Jehoshaphat and the people went out to battle. However, the strategy was quite different. Instead of putting his best soldiers up front, armed and ready, he chose musicians and singers to lead the army to battle. They remembered that Judah meant *"Praise."* They knew of their inheritance ordained by God through their father Jacob.

Genesis 49:8-10: Judah, thou art he whom thy brethren shall praise: thy hand shall be in the neck of thine enemies; thy father's children shall bow down before thee.

The tribe of Judah was to be victorious and successful in war: **Thy hand shall be in the neck of thy enemies.** *God always reveals figuratively in the natural what He will do spiritually.* He ordained Praise through the tribe of Judah. It was established that in battle, Judah would always go first.

Judges 1:1-4: Now after the death of Joshua it came to pass, that the children of Israel asked the LORD, saying, Who shall go up for us against the Canaanites first, to fight against them?

2   *And the LORD said, Judah shall go up: behold, I have delivered the land into his hand.*

3   *And Judah said unto Simeon his brother, Come up with me into my lot, that we may fight against the Canaanites; and I likewise will go with thee into thy lot. So Simeon went with him.*

4   *And Judah went up; and the LORD delivered the Canaanites and the Perizzites into their hand: and they slew of them in Bezek ten thousand men. (KJV)*

Judah was the principal leading tribe out of all the tribes of Israel designated as the source of God's power since this is where His presence dwell. Judah was God's sanctuary—His home. It was His sacred dwelling-place. Judah was recognized as the tribe where power was to be concentrated, and from which the Messiah was to proceed.

Ps 114:1-2: When Israel came out of Egypt, the house of Jacob from a people of foreign tongue, Judah became God's sanctuary, Israel his dominion. (NIV)

God inhabits the praises of His people (**Psalms 22:3**). Praise brings God on the scene. When Judah went first, there was always victory. When you offer up the sacrifice of praise in the midst of your circumstances, God arises on your behalf to see you through.

The men of Moab and Ammon made one grave error. They tried to contend against Judah. The devil cannot stand against praise for in praise is the power of God to deliver and destroy the works of the enemy. It's like a burglar trying to break into a house when the owner is home and is well armed with automatic weapons. Believe me, he will get more than he bargained for.

As Judah went forth in praise, singing, *"Praise Ye the Lord for His mercy endures forever and ever!"* God caused the enemies of Jehoshaphat to fight and destroy each another. As they approached the scene of the battle, they found their enemies dead bodies along with all the riches and material things they had brought to battle with them. It took the kingdom of Judah three whole days to bring back the spoils to the city. *When praise goes forth, not only is the enemy destroyed, but you will pick up the spoils also!* The people assembled in the valley of *Berachah,* which means *blessings or prosperity. Praise will move us out of the valley of darkness, debt, despair, desperation into the valley of promise—God's promises which are yes and Amen.* So not only is the power of God released through praise, blessings will also follow the one who lifts up the Father in adoration.

2 Corinthians 1:20:For all the promises of God in him are yea, and in him Amen, unto the glory of God by us.

In the military, after a major operation, we would designate a rally point to assemble together and ensure that everyone was all right. Where do you want to assemble today? Do you want to stay in your despair and lack, or do you want to assemble in the valley of Berachah—the place of blessings? The choice is yours today. Let the praises of God go before you each day to defeat the devil in his operations against you. Don't wait until the circumstances pile up. Live a life of praise. With praise as your weapon, no weapon formed against you will prosper. Though the devil may come like a flood, as you raise up a standard of praise against him (**Isaiah 59:15**), he is defeated and the spoils are yours to keep!

CHAPTER FOUR

▼

THE NAMES FOR PRAISE

In the final chapter of Psalms, David urges the Levites to exercise their liberty in praising the Lord. This psalm was primarily intended for the Levites, to stir them up to do their office in the house of the Lord, as singers and players on instruments. Today, we must receive it as speaking to us, who are now God's spiritual priests.

Psalms 150:1-6

1   *Praise ye the LORD. Praise God in his sanctuary: praise him in the firmament of his power.*

2   *Praise him for his mighty acts: praise him according to his excellent greatness.*

3   *Praise him with the sound of the trumpet: praise him with the psaltery and harp.*

4   *Praise him with the timbrel and dance: praise him with stringed instruments and organs.*

5   *Praise him upon the loud cymbals: praise him upon the high*
       sounding cymbals.
6   *Let every thing that hath breath praise the LORD. Praise ye the*
       LORD.

We are to praise Him in the sanctuary, the temple. This denotes that we
are to praise God in the congregation of the saints in the place designated
such as the church. This is not a private matter as some people think.
Some religious people think praise is some subdued, private, ritual
between them and God. ***Praise Him in the Sanctuary!*** In the firmament
of His power—His power is in the earth. Praise Him for His mighty
acts—the things He has done for you and others. Our praise is a testimony of the goodness, the grace, the glory, and the power of our God.

The Psalmist continues to exhort us to praise by appealing to us to use
every instrument and voice to praise God with every breath, every essence
of our being, and with a melodious heart. We are to praise Him with a
strong faith that God will deliver us in times of peril. Our praise to Him
should be a response with a holy love, great delight, and with sincerity of
heart. We are to enjoy ourselves in His presence as a cheerful child in submission to His will and with expectation of one day abiding with Him in
His kingdom.

NAMES FOR PRAISE

"Brother Jones, you keep telling me to "Praise the Lord," and I want to, but
what exactly does "Praise the Lord" means? You know, I am glad you asked
that. There are several Hebrew and Greek translations for the word,
"Praise." Each one describes the different ways we may express our praise
to God. Each manifestation reaches God in different ways and has a specific function.

Some of the functions of praise are to refresh, to instruct, to strengthen, to minister effectively, to empower, and to release spiritual gifts. The word, *"praise"* used here in Psalms 150, comes from the Hebrew word, *"halal"* which **means** *to make a show, to boast; and thus to be (clamorously) foolish; to rave; and to celebrate.* Other definitions include *to celebrate, commend, to give oneself in marriage, sing, [be worthy of] praise, rage, and to shine.*

We should be excited about our God to the point that we should declare to world emphatically our love for Him. A fanatic is an ardent (passionate, emotional) devotee, having an excessive zeal or an irrational attachment for a cause or a person. Remember **Isaiah 43:21** that says we were created by God to demonstrate His praise. Well, who wants something no one else wants. When we are excited about God and display a love for Him that surpasses human intellect, people will want what we have. There are people who are going through bad marriages that long for the relationship they may see in another couple. Well, Halal means we are joined in marriage to God. It's like a honeymoon that never ends. It's okay to shout, be happy, and just get beside yourself as you praise the Father.

Now understand, all things must be done decent and in order. If you are praising God in the Spirit, it will be. **Psalms 69: 30, 31,** says praise will please God more than your sacrifices (your works). I ran into a religious group that was more into works than praise. They told me that I wasn't supposed to get too excited about God. I told them that when I think of the goodness of my God and what He had done for me, that it was like fire shut up in my bones and I have to shout, dance, and bless His name. I started getting excited in front of them and they panicked, saying, "Brother Ken, please calm down." I couldn't and those spirits surrounding them got so scared and restless that they started for the door, but I just kept on shouting until they were gone. I was raised in a religion that you couldn't say "Amen," unless it was under your breath. Well, never again. I will praise with all of my heart and soul while I have my being!

Another name for praise is the word, **"Yadah"** (Ya-daw) which means *to revere or worship with extended hands.* The lifting up of hands is essential in praise. Paul says in **1 Timothy 2:8** that he wished that all men should pray (worship), lifting up holy hands without wrath and doubting. When we lift our hands, we show *volitional surrender unto God.* This means that it is an act of our will when we praise God. Whenever you see someone being held up or robbed, the first thing the victim does is raise his or her hands. That means that all they possess is for the taking. When we lift our hands to God the Father, all that we have, all that we possess should belong to Him. God wants our hearts, not our possessions for He knows if He gains our hearts, everything else will follow. Praise is an act of the heart, mind, the will, and the emotions.

"Tehillah"(the-hil-lah) **is a sacred ode (poem) accompanied by voice, harp, or instrument of music.** It is a hymn, a laudation that is sung to the Lord that increases our faith, our confidence, and our commitment. **Psalms 65:1**: *"Praise waiteth for thee, O God, in Sion: and unto thee shall the vow be performed."* God is deserving of our praise and it is fitting that we praise Him. **Colossians 3:16** and **Ephesians 5:19** admonishes us to train and encourage one another with psalms, hymns, and spiritual songs. A *psalm,* as we know is a poem set to music as we see in the book of Psalms. A *hymn* is a song that is song by a person that encourages us by their faith and endurance through trials and joys. *Spiritual songs* are stronger in doctrine, prophetic, and teaching.

One of the functions of praise is to teach. We use music today, to influence thoughts, actions, and attitudes of the people who hear them. Every generation is known by the music they regard. So it is so important that the church give heed to what is sung in the church. Songs of defeat will leave people feeling defeated. Hymns of faith, strength, courage, and joy will strengthen the resolve of those who hear it. Paul is saying that we have the ability to teach and pass ideas onto others through song. We are to excite and encourage one another while at the same time, convey instructions to one another.

That is why we should sing the Word. There are a lot of songs out there that are sung that are not according to scripture. That is why so many saints are defeated. They enjoy some of these emotional songs, but are not strengthened because there is no word in them. Finally, no song or hymn is perfected unless we sing it with grace and melody in our heart, being truly affected by the words we sing.

My favorite word for praise is **"Shabach"** (Shaw-bak), meaning *a loud, sustaining noise; a loud tone; a voice of triumph.* When I received the Baptism of the Holy Spirit, these were the first two syllables I could speak. I believe that as God was filling me with the Spirit, He was calling and anointing me as a minister of praise and worship. There are times in my life, I get stressed and the only release I get is when I just shout to the Lord in one loud, continuous note. Joshua brought down the walls of Jericho with a loud shout and obtained the victory from God over the enemy.

Joshua 6:5: *"And it shall come to pass, that when they make a long blast with the ram's horn, and when ye hear the sound of the trumpet, all the people shall shout with a great shout; and the wall of the city shall fall down flat, and the people shall ascend up every man straight before him."*

The word, "shout" from the word, *"ruwa" (roo-ah') means, to split the ears (with sound), i.e. (shout for alarm or joy); make a joyful noise, smart, shout (for joy), sound an alarm, triumph.* The city of Jericho was a walled city. It was a stronghold that had to be destroyed so that Joshua and the children of Israel could enter into the Promised Land. **2nd Corinthians 10:4** says, *"For the weapons of our warfare are not carnal, but mighty through God to the pulling down of strong holds".* A stronghold is any thought, imagination, or argument that usurps itself over the knowledge of God and gains a *strong hold* on our minds. I mentioned several times that Praise is a weapon in our war against the devil. As soon as impure, evil, or fleshly thoughts enter our mind, we refute, pull down, and destroy them, by shouting unto God with a voice of triumph (praise). Just as Joshua and his men were able to ascend upon every man in the city once the walls fell flat, so will the believer's thoughts ascend over the enemy's as we stay in a praise attitude. The next time you are going through some tough times, just try it and shout unto the Lord with a loud, sustaining noise. It will, as some say, "Clear your head."

Contrary to some religious beliefs, the use of instruments to accompany praise is essential. **"Zamar"**(Zaw-mar) is another name for praise meaning **to *touch the strings of a musical instrument; to play upon or to make music accompanied by voice; and to celebrate in music and song (Psalms 108:1-3).*** Another function of praise is to bring refreshment to our souls and to open our spirits so as to receive from God. In **2nd Kings 3:15,** Elisha required a minstrel to play for him to refresh his soul so that he could hear from God.

15   *But now bring me a minstrel. And it came to pass, when the minstrel played, that the hand of the LORD came upon him.*

Music was a regular accompaniment of prophecy. The school of the prophets would play the harp, lyre, and tambourine as they prophesied. As the minstrel played for Elisha, his mind became calm and sedate and he was able to bring forth the Word of God to those who were inquiring. David used the harp to bring refreshment to Saul when the evil spirit troubled him.

1 Sam 16:23: *"And it came to pass, when the evil spirit from God was upon Saul, that David took an harp, and played with his hand: so Saul was refreshed, and was well, and the evil spirit departed from him."*

To hear God's praises sweetly sung would cheer Saul's spirit, and settle his mind, and help to put him into a right spirit both to speak to and to hear from God. Many times we just need to get quiet before the Lord and allow spiritual praise, sung with music, to relax us so that we can hear His still, small, voice and receive guidance, instruction, and direction for our lives.

"**Hilluwl**" (hil-lool) is *a celebration of thanksgiving for harvest; to be merry.* Just as the angels rejoice when one soul is saved, we should rejoice as we reap souls for the kingdom of God and receive the blessings that He has bestowed on us.

"**Towdah**" (to-dah) **means to worship with extended, open hands.** As you can see, the movement of the body is important is praise. It is hard to praise without some type of exuberance, movement, and emotion. When we kneel before God in reverence and bless Him as an act of adoration, then we "**Barak**" Him. **This type of praise involves kneeling before God as a gesture of reverence, obedience, or respect.** We bless or commend God in adoration for what He has done in our lives and for who He is.

There are other forms of expression by which we praise God. *Dancing* is also an integral part of our praise service. *It is the rhythmic movement of the body, usually done or performed to musical accompaniment.* Among the Jews, dancing generally occurred among women, either singly or in a group. It was a way of celebrating joyous occasions. Indeed, dancing became a symbol of joy, the opposite of mourning (Ps. 30:11; Eccl. 3:4; Luke 15:25). One of the mightiest men of battle also danced in his praise to God.

2 Sam 6:14: *"And David danced before the LORD with all his might; and David was girded with a linen ephod."*

Dancing should be the order of the day when we enter His gates with thanksgiving in our hearts and His courts with praise (Psalms 100:4).

Praising God for who He is called *adoration*. Praising Him for what He does is known as *thanksgiving*. Our Praise of God may be in song or prayer, individually or collectively, spontaneous or prearranged, originating from the emotions or from our will with sincere intentions. **Psalms 108:1-5** provides us an outline for the conduct of praise in our lives.

Psalms 108:1-5

1   O God, my heart is fixed; I will sing and give praise, even with my glory.

2   Awake, psaltery and harp: I myself will awake early.

3   I will praise thee, O LORD, among the people: and I will sing praises unto thee among the nations.

4   For thy mercy is great above the heavens: and thy truth reacheth unto the clouds.

5   Be thou exalted, O God, above the heavens: and thy glory above all the earth;

We must praise God with fixedness of heart. Our whole heart and soul must be employed in the duty of the service. David tells his soul in **Psalms 103:1**, to bless the Lord, affectionately and that all that is within him bless His holy name. Wandering and straggling thoughts must be gathered in and our focus should be on Him. Second, we must praise God with freeness of expression. **Psalms 57:8** says our tongue is our glory and should be consecrated in its use in praise. We should praise God with liberty, using instruments of praise, dancing, and delighting ourselves in Him.

Finally, we must praise God with fervency of affection and stir up ourselves to do it that it may be done in a lively manner, yet not carelessly. There must also be a public expression of our praise. We should not be ashamed to recognize Him publicly and should encourage others to do the same. The way we praise the Father is important. Whether with outstretched hands, dancing, shouting, or singing with instruments, God is pleased as we worship Him with our most important asset—our heart.

CHAPTER FIVE

▼

WORSHIP SUSTAINETH THEE

You have received a lot of knowledge concerning praise in this book. That is why it is appropriately called, "Praise Goeth Before Thee." Yet, it would be difficult not to provide any teachings concerning Worship. Many people think that they are the same. Some ignorantly think the "worship service," is coming to church, hear a few selections, pay their tithes and offering, pay their respects to God, hear the sermon, and go home.

Just as praise strengthens us and bolsters our faith and confidence in God for what He has done and is about to do, worship sustains our relationship with Him. It allows us to have intimate contact with God.

Ps 103:7: He made known his ways unto Moses, his acts unto the children of Israel.

Ps 95:10: Forty years long was I grieved with this generation, and said, It is a people that do err in their heart, and they have not known my ways:

The word, **"acts"** comes from the Hebrew word, *'aliylah* (al-ee-law'), *meaning an exploit (of God), or a performance (of man, often in a bad sense), by implication, an opportunity.*

The children of God knew God acts. **Psalms 150:2** says, *"Praise him for his mighty acts: praise him according to his excellent greatness."* We praise the Father for the things He has done and in response to His acts of greatness. There is nothing wrong with this. However, it limits the relationship one has with God. If you only get caught up in the acts, then your faith, your lifestyle, and your character will be like a roller coaster. That is how some Christians live their lives, up and down, depending upon the circumstances in their lives. As soon as Israel forgot the acts, their hearts turned again.

Numbers 11:1 *And when the people complained, it displeased the LORD: and the LORD heard it; and his anger was kindled; and the fire of the LORD burnt among them, and consumed them that were in the uttermost parts of the camp.*

If you only get caught up in the acts, then you will be unstable, unreliable, and unproductive. Another definition mentioned regarding "acts" talks about *the performances of man.* It is so unfortunate that many people (especially religious people) can get so caught up in the performances of men and not of God. There are many singers out there who lifestyles do not line up with the Word of God, yet people get excited about them and their songs. But their songs don't last in their spirits because what they have may be wrapped in gospel, but without substance and power. People get emotional and sometimes comforted by these songs, but they are not sustained.

In Exodus, the 32d chapter, the children of Israel, fearing that Moses had left them alone in the wilderness, persuaded Aaron to make them a new god to worship. You see, if you only get caught up in the acts, you may never develop a relationship that will stand in faith. The first thing the Israelites did after they convinced Aaron to make a golden calf for their worship was to have a service for it and begin to play.

Exodus 32:6 "And they rose up early on the morrow, and offered burnt offerings, and brought peace offerings; and the people sat down to eat and to drink, and rose up to play."

In **Exodus 32:7**, God said they have corrupted themselves. Every time we lean on the arm of flesh, we corrupt ourselves. The flesh, like all organic materials, will one day decay. When we trust, lean on, and respond in the flesh, we only set ourselves up for decay. The precepts of men, rituals, and tradition eat away at our spirits, and erode our relationship with the Father God.

I spoke with a young man one day on an airplane flying home. He was going to a "Worship Seminar." He said that many churches use these seminars as a way to teach new songs, but very little time is given to actual teaching concerning praise and worship. These seminars also do not address the lifestyles of the people who sing. The young man was disappointed because he said when going to these seminars, he would run into two spirits: homosexuality and promiscuity (uncontrolled sexual appetites). When I was in college, I was a member of Students for Christ. It was a Christian organization that came out of a certain denomination that was established on the campus. One of the reasons we broke away, was because of the denomination that was there was so corrupt that we just couldn't co-exist.

Their choir was on their way to a retreat one weekend. The president of the organization did a "shake down" on the bus prior to leaving. You see this choir had a reputation, although it was a "church choir" for being some of the biggest sinners on campus. It reeked of homosexuality, whoremongers, and substance abusers. Well, when the president did the shake down, he found drugs and alcohol throughout the bus. And they were going on a retreat! Oh, did I mention they could sing like angels, but they lived like devils. Do not trust in the performance of man. Allow your praise to rest in the hands of God.

I know what I just said was hard, but I'm tired of people playing church. We have people who need a touch from God, need victory in their lives, and to be ministered to. They need the real thing and not a facsimile (fake product).

The children of Israel knew the exploits of God and they praised Him. *Moses knew God ways, and he worshipped Him. God made known His ways to Moses through intimate fellowship with Him.* Moses had a worship relationship with the Father based upon an intimate knowledge with Him.

So there is a difference between worship and praise. Worship comes from several Hebrew words, just as praise, but the meanings are different.

Psalms 5:7 But as for me, I will come into thy house in the multitude of thy mercy: and in thy fear will I worship toward thy holy temple.

Worship, here is defined, *"shachah"* (shaw-khaw') which means **to depress, to lay prostrate in homage to royalty or God.** It also means to **bow (self) down, crouch, fall down (flat), humbly beseech, do (make) obeisance, do reverence, make to stoop, and to worship.** Worship is also used synonymous with the word, "Fear," as stated in the Hebrew, *"yir'ah"* (yir-aw') meaning morally, reverence.

Psalms 111:10 The fear of the LORD is the beginning of wisdom: a good understanding have all they that do his commandments: his praise endureth for ever.
Ps 34:9: O fear the LORD, ye his saints: for there is no want to them that fear him.

Notice that there are blessings associated with worship. Many times, people seek the provisions and the gifts. Yet, if they would only seek and worship the *"Provider"*, the provisions would come; if they would worship the *"Giver"* the gifts would come.

The fear of the Lord is the beginning of Wisdom. We can obtain wisdom for our lives as we spend time in the presence of God, worshipping Him. God's presence will energize our minds to understand His divine purpose and how to handle the things we face in life. **Colossians 2:3**, says, *"In whom are hid all the treasures of wisdom and knowledge."* You do not have to go around asking people to pray for you that God would give you wisdom. Get into the presence of God and worship Him.

Everything you need is in the presence of God. I had someone ask me to pray for them that God give them strength. "Pray for my strength, Bro. Jones." I told this person to get in the presence of God. I explained that **Psalms 16:11** says, "in His presence is fullness of Joy." And **Nehemiah 8:10** says, *"for the joy of the LORD is your strength."* Therefore in His presence is fullness of strength. Stop looking for shortcuts around the throne and go to it!

The word, "Seek" is also used in the bible to denote worship. Seek in the Hebrew means **to pursue or search; to worship; to diligently inquire or frequent; and to seek or ask.**

2 Chronicles 14:4: *"And commanded Judah to seek the LORD God of their fathers, and to do the law and the commandment."*

Psalms 105:4: *"Seek the LORD, and his strength: seek his face forevermore."*

As believers, we should long for God's presence. David says *"As the hart (deer) panteth after the water brooks, so panteth my soul after thee, O God."* **(Psalms 42:1)** It is said of the hart that he has a small stomach and must continually be around the water (the source) in order to survive. We must continually be in God's presence in order to survive spiritually. Our longing should be just like the deer, a dry, panting want for God's presence. We satisfy this requirement through Worship.

Worship in the Greek means, *proskuneo* (pros-koo-neh'-o) meaning *to kiss, like a dog licking his master's hand; to fawn or crouch to, to literally or figuratively, prostrate oneself in homage (do reverence to, adore).*

Revelation 15:4: *"Who shall not fear thee, O Lord, and glorify thy name? for thou only art holy: for all nations shall come and worship before thee; for thy judgments are made manifest."*

It is the same worship that Jesus mentions in **John 4:24:**

John 4:24: *"God is a Spirit: and they that worship him must worship him in spirit and in truth."*

Many of us can quote this scripture. It relates to the conversation that Jesus had with the Samaritan woman at the well (**John 4:20-24**). He told her that the Samaritans did not know what they were worshiping. *You see, without a revealed knowledge of Christ that comes through spending time with Him, you can not truly worship Him.* He also told her about her lifestyle that she was living with a man that was not her husband. We serve a holy God, therefore, our lives must be holy as well in order to be a pleasing sacrifice unto Him. God will not drink from a dirty vessel. So our worship to Him is enhanced by our way of life and godly lifestyle.

Finally, He told her that they that worship God must worship Him in spirit and truth. *In spirit, means fervency and genuineness of heart.* The true worshippers, all, who truly and sincerely worship God, do it with the heart, and not merely in form as some do. God is not pleased when our lips do not line up with our heart. God is a spirit. That means that we must worship Him in spirit in order to reach Him. He is seeking true worshipers today. Are you one of them?

Isaiah 29:13 "Wherefore the Lord said, Forasmuch as this people draw near me with their mouth, and with their lips do honour me, but have removed their heart far from me, and their fear toward me is taught by the precept of men."

Tradition and religion dampens our relationship with God, and hinders true worship. When we worship God in spirit, He is touched by our heartfelt emotion.

To worship in truth means to worship Him in accordance to His word. Jesus said, in **John 17:17,** *"Sanctify them through thy truth: thy word is truth."* We need to understand what God says about worship in His word and not go after the dictates of men.

There is an another difference between praise and worship. Many people can start a relationship, but have trouble maintaining it. We can get excited about God in praise, but the minute someone calls for worship, we shy away. This is because the more you become intimate with someone, the more exposed you are to them. People do not like that. Worship is a relationship builder by which we come to know God intimately and worship Him because of it.

Praise will bring you to your feet. Worship will bring you to His Feet. Praise is Excited Faith. Worship is Knowing Faith.

We have the opportunity to be familiar with God's ways and His mighty acts. Allow praise and worship to be an essential part of your daily walk with God. Praise will stimulate your faith and keep you focused on God's hand in your life. Worship will allow you to be sensitive to the touch of the Father's hand as you walk in communion with Him, building on your love relationship with Him. There is power in Praise and there is intimacy in worship. Become a true worshipper today as Jesus spoke of in John, chapter 4. Know whom it is you worship and worship Him in spirit and truth.

CHAPTER SIX

▼

OUR FIRST MINISTRY

One of the most inspiring stories in the New Testament that talks about our commitment to worship and praise is found in Luke 10:38-42.

Luke 10:38-42

38 Now it came to pass, as they went, that he entered into a certain village: and a certain woman named Martha received him into her house.

39 And she had a sister called Mary, which also sat at Jesus' feet, and heard his word.

40 But Martha was cumbered about much serving, and came to him, and said, Lord, dost thou not care that my sister hath left me to serve alone? bid her therefore that she help me.

41 And Jesus answered and said unto her, Martha, Martha, thou art careful and troubled about many things:

42 But one thing is needful: and Mary hath chosen that good part, which shall not be taken away from her.

Many of us know the story of Mary and Martha. Martha welcomed Jesus into her home and she and her sister, Mary, served him. Although many criticized Martha, one cannot deny the fact, that she welcomed Jesus. However, Martha was "distracted" with too much serving and was angry with her sister, Mary, who chose to sit at the feet of Jesus and hear His words. She complained to Jesus, wondering if He cared that she was doing all the work while Mary did nothing. Jesus responded that Martha was too concerned about too many things and that Mary had chosen that "best part" which would not be taken from her.

If you read the scripture, it doesn't say that Mary did not work or serve Jesus, for she did. Also, Martha did sit at Jesus' feet. Mary knew her first ministry was to the Lord. As I said earlier, some people are caught up in the *work of the Lord and not the worship of the Lord or as some say being caught up in the work of the Lord and not the Lord of the work.* If you allow yourself to get too caught up in "Works," you will become too distracted in your relationship with the Lord. The "cares of the world," will slowly creep in and your worship unto the Lord will dwindle. You will lose that freshness and comfort that comes from spending time in God's presence.

The early church knew of the importance of ministering unto the Lord as their utmost priority.

Acts 13:2 As they ministered to the Lord, and fasted, the Holy Ghost said, Separate me Barnabas and Saul for the work whereunto I have called them.

As they committed themselves first unto the ministry of praise and worship, God empowered them to go forth and do the work. *Worship before Works; Prayer before Works; Salvation before Works, Relationship before Works.* Am I making myself clear on this matter?

RESULTS OF WORSHIP:

As you put God first and worship Him, you will see a greater operation of the Spirit in your life. God is looking for true worshippers for whom He can show Himself strong in their behalf (John 4:23; 2Chronicles 16:9). Thus, there are many benefits and blessings to be gained through worship. As we said earlier, worship brings God on the scene. He desires to be with us, as we should desire to be with Him. As we come to know Him, our relationship is strengthened and so is our faith. That is why worship is so important as to increase our knowledge of Him in spiritual understanding of who He really is and His great love for us.

Worship leads to revelation and that revelation causes us to worship the Lord even more. As we worship the Father, He reveals Himself to us so much the more and we are able to grasp with more clarity, who our Father really is. As we come into a revelation knowledge of the Father, it encourages us to worship Him in response to a greater understanding of His goodness, glory, power, and honor. It is true to say, that those who have problems with worship have problems with their knowledge of God. Our greatest desire should be to know the Father and to continually inquire of Him for a more intimate relationship. Our intimacy increases with a greater knowledge of the love of God.

Philippians 3:10 "I want to know Christ and the power of his resurrection and the fellowship of sharing in his sufferings, becoming like him in his death,"(NIV)
Psalms 27:4 "One thing have I desired of the LORD, that will I seek after; that I may dwell in the house of the LORD all the days of my life, to behold the beauty of the LORD, and to inquire in his temple."(KJV)

Worship brings us into one accord and in unity of the Spirit. Throughout the bible, as the people came together in one accord to worship the Father, they were united as one with Him. God's power flows as we are united and the anointing is released to meet the needs of the people gathered before Him.

Ps 133:1-3 "Behold, how good and how pleasant it is for brethren to dwell together in unity!
2   It is like the precious ointment upon the head, that ran down upon the beard, even Aaron's beard: that went down to the skirts of his garments;
3   As the dew of Hermon, and as the dew that descended upon the mountains of Zion: for there the LORD commanded the blessing, even life for evermore." (KJV)

Worship Releases the Power of God. As we said earlier, Worship opens up a portal by which the Father can minister unto us individually and corporately. Just as we have studied about praise, worship gets God's attention and His power is released in abundance to work out His will for our lives. As the church comes together in unity, as mentioned in the 133d chapter of Psalms, an ointment which is representative of the Holy Spirit (the anointing), is released and the blessings of God will begin to flow.

2 Chronicles 5:13-14 "It came even to pass, as the trumpeters and singers were as one, to make one sound to be heard in praising and thanking the LORD; and when they lifted up their voice with the trumpets and cymbals and instruments of musick, and praised the LORD, saying, For he is good; for his mercy endureth for ever: that then the house was filled with a cloud, even the house of the LORD;
14   So that the priests could not stand to minister by reason of the cloud: for the glory of the LORD had filled the house of God." (KJV)

Once again, we see how worship, together in unity, brings down the presence of God. That is why it is vital for the church to come into the knowledge of true praise and worship, so that the congregation will be blessed as a whole from the presence of God. I'm not talking about some fleshly, screaming, out of control ordeal. I'm talking about God coming down and taking over the service, rejoicing with us and ministering to our every need.

I pray that you come into intimate knowledge of the Father through worship and establish your relationship with Him. All that you need is in His presence, so seek Him as your required need today. An opportunity for you to come into closer fellowship with the Lord awaits you. Worship is your relationship builder. Come to know God's ways as well as His acts. Your faith will be strengthened, your walk steadied, and your power increased. Worship is the key to the heart of the Father. Don't neglect such an opportunity.

CHAPTER SEVEN

▼

GOD'S PRESCRIBED ORDER

Many people believe that the praise and worship service is one big free for all in which anything goes. Others believe that it doesn't matter what songs they sing or how the....worship service it is conducted, just as long as everyone participates. If you believe that then you are wrong. God has provided the Holy Spirit to assist us in our worship of the Father. There is at times, specific instructions by which we are to worship God to achieve the results we desire in our services. I believe that God has a prescribed order for worship.

1 Chronicles 15:12,13 (King David is speaking to the Levites) "And said unto them, Ye are the chief of the fathers of the Levites: sanctify yourselves, both ye and your brethren, that ye may bring up the ark of the LORD God of Israel unto the place that I have prepared for it.
13 For because ye did it not at the first, the LORD our God made a breach upon us, for that we sought him not after the due order. (KJV)

This is an interesting story about David and the lesson he learned about the prescribed order in praise and worship. I am not trying to be legalistic about praise and worship. Although it is true that both praise and worship comes from the heart, we cannot neglect the principle that God does everything decent and in order. I've been in services where people got so emotionally wrought that they ran out the building, ran through solid wood doors, even injuring themselves. There must be direction and guidance given to corporate praise and worship so that God can effectively minister unto His people. It is very critical for the praise leader to be in tuned with the Holy Spirit to receive instruction and lead the people into the presence of God. Once in His presence, it is imperative that God is allowed to move by His Spirit freely and without hindrance.

1 Chronicles 13:1-4: And David consulted with the captains of thousands and hundreds, and with every leader.

2   *And David said unto all the congregation of Israel, If it seem good unto you, and that it be of the LORD our God, let us send abroad unto our brethren every where, that are left in all the land of Israel, and with them also to the priests and Levites which are in their cities and suburbs, that they may gather themselves unto us:*

3   *And let us bring again the ark of our God to us: for we inquired not at it in the days of Saul.*

4   *And all the congregation said that they would do so: for the thing was right in the eyes of all the people. (KJV)*

David and the congregation desired to have the ark of God brought to them so that God's presence would be with them. However, David missed God in bringing up the Ark of the Covenant. He had good intentions of bringing the ark back to Jerusalem, but he got too overzealous and wanted to do things in a grand, spectacular, way.

1 Chronicles 13:7 "And they carried the ark of God in a new cart out of the house of Abinadab: and Uzza and Ahio drave the cart"(KJV)

God had instructed the Israelites to bring up the Ark of the Covenant using poles and that only the priests could carry the ark. There was to be no deviation from this commandment.

Numbers 7:9 But unto the sons of Kohath he gave none: because the service of the sanctuary belonging unto them was that they should bear upon their shoulders. (KJV)

David knew that the Levites were to carry the ark upon their shoulders. None ought to carry the ark but the Levites. The Kohathites carried it in their ordinary marches, and therefore had no wagons allotted them, because their work was to bear the ark upon their shoulders. However, upon extraordinary occasions, as when they passed Jordan and compassed Jericho, the priests carried it. This rule was plain and explicit, and yet David himself forgot it, and put the ark upon a cart.

1 Chronicles 15:15 "And the children of the Levites bare the ark of God upon their shoulders with the staves thereon, as Moses commanded according to the word of the LORD."

As I said before, it was a commandment of the Lord. But David had another idea. He thought it would be grander to place the ark on a new cart pulled by oxen. You can be sincere in doing things for God, but you can be sincerely wrong, especially in this case.

1 Chronicles 13:8-13

8   *And David and all Israel played before God with all their might, and with singing, and with harps, and with psalteries, and with timbrels, and with cymbals, and with trumpets.*

9   *And when they came unto the threshingfloor of Chidon, Uzza put forth his hand to hold the ark; for the oxen stumbled.*

10   *And the anger of the LORD was kindled against Uzza, and he smote him, because he put his hand to the ark: and there he died before God.*

11   *And David was displeased, because the LORD had made a breach upon Uzza: wherefore that place is called Perezuzza to this day.*

12   *And David was afraid of God that day, saying, How shall I bring the ark of God home to me?*

13   *So David brought not the ark home to himself to the city of David, but carried it aside into the house of Obededom the Gittite*

14   *And the ark of God remained with the family of Obededom in his house three months. And the LORD blessed the house of Obededom, and all that he had. (KJV)*

As they proceeded with the ark towards Jerusalem, the cart hit a bump. Uzzah, who had been in charge of the ark, tried to steady it. This angered God and He struck Uzzah dead. David was both angry and afraid. He left the ark with Obed-Edom, who was actually responsible for the ark. While in his presence, his (Obed-Edom) household prospered.

The ark represents the presence of God. We have to be serious when handling and when ministering in the presence of God. Good intentions, bells and whistles, and great performances do not please God—only obedience that stems from a broken and contrite heart. I believe that Uzzah got a little "too familiar" with the ark thinking highly of himself. He felt that since he was driving the wagon, that he had the authority to touch the ark. Unfortunately, God humbled him with his death. We cannot allow ourselves to become irreverent in God's presence. Some churches reduce Christ to a "Rock Star," shouting and ranting like they are at a worldly concert. Believe me, God is definitely, "Not in the House."

When David got his act together in 1 Chronicles 15th Chapter, he was able to bring up the Ark of the Covenant in the due order that God had prescribed. *There is victory, power, release of the Spirit, when we worship God according to the due order.* While the ark was in the household of Obed-Edom, he prospered because he knew how to handle the ark. He was assigned to care for the Ark of the Lord, therefore he was sensitive to its needs. As leaders, more importantly, song leaders, we should be skillful in operating in the presence of God so that we can be successful in ministering to others, following the flow or leading of God's Spirit.

1 Chronicles 15:13: For because ye did it not at the first, the LORD our God made a breach upon us, for that we sought him not after the due order.

The key to understanding God's divine order for praise and worship is to know what God desires in His Word and to be attentive to the Holy Spirit.

1 Corinthians 2:10-11
10   But God hath revealed them unto us by his Spirit: for the Spirit searcheth all things, yea, the deep things of God.
11   For what man knoweth the things of a man, save the spirit of man which is in him? even so the things of God knoweth no man, but the Spirit of God.

It is the Spirit of God, who always operate in line with the Word of God, and who knows the mind of God. Following the leading of the Holy Ghost then is essential in understanding God's divine order. Besides, it is God's praise so He should know how He wants it. So much praise and worship today is man led, man driven, man inspired, and mandated from religion and ceremony without any guidance from the Father.

1 Chronicles 15:26 And it came to pass, when God helped the Levites that bare the ark of the covenant of the LORD, that they offered seven bullocks and seven rams.

The Holy Spirit will help us to enter into God's presence if we are obedient to His will and praise and worship Him in the proper order or manner. God does everything *"decent and in order" (Well formed and in proper arrangement). We need God's help in order for our praise and worship to be of any use to Him and a blessing to others. "The Levites, remembering the breach upon Uzza, were probably ready to tremble when they took up the ark; but God helped them, that is, he encouraged them through it, silenced their fears, and strengthened their faith. God helped them to do it decently and well, and without making any mistake. If we perform any religious duties so as to escape a breach, and come off with our lives, we must glory in the fact that it is God that helps us; for, if left to ourselves, we should be guilty of some fatal miscarriages. God's ministers that bear the vessels of the Lord have special need of divine help in their ministrations so that God in them may be glorified and his church edified. And, if God help the Levites, the people have the benefit of it"* (**Matthew Commentary**)

DOING ALL THINGS WELL

David, after finally getting it right the second time, rejoiced and began to remember what God had taught Him from the scriptures. Several things took place. First, ***David ranked ordered the Levites and assigned them responsibilities. There must be structure in the church to minister effectively.*** The presence of God is not manifested by accident. David instituted praise in his tabernacle. Before this, in the Tabernacle of Moses, there was no praise. So David appointed the Levites to sing and minister before the Lord in music and song. They were instructed to petition God, give thanks, sing joyful songs and play skillfully before

God. He appointed Chenaniah, who was skillful in song to be the song leader and teach others regarding the matters of the song. I believe this was more than just lyrics, but how to effectively minister unto the Lord in praise. We have to be taught. Too many churches ignore this and wonder why they do not see the manifest presence of God in their services. Not an emotional "wingding" but the presence of God.

They consecrated themselves for the service. (1 Chronicles 15:12) No *one should minister before God unless they are consecrated, sanctified, and prepared for service.* The word, "consecrate," *means to set apart for service.* We must set ourselves apart from worldly influences and sin to be effective in ministering to God. We are required by God to consecrate ourselves (**Romans 12:1; 2 Tim. 2:21**). One of the results of our consecration by Christ is that we have become a priesthood of believers (**1 Pet. 2:9**) with direct access to our heavenly Father (**Ephesians. 3:11-12**). The priests in 1 Chronicles, 15th chapter, had to consecrate themselves in order to bring up the ark or the presence of the Lord.

After praise went before the ark and it was set inside the tent, David blessed the people and distributed to them a loaf of bread and cakes of raisins and dates. When God's presence is in place, then it is time to bless the people and minister unto their needs. As David found joy in ministering unto the Lord, he took time to minister unto others. We incorporate the presence of God in our lives so that we can effectively minister unto His people.

David left Asaph and several of the priests to minister daily and regularly before the Lord. Burnt offerings and petitions were made morning and evening. Hence, praise is a lifestyle for the believer and not just a Sunday morning experience. We are to be God-conscious and seek His face daily. It was expected of everyone involved on our Praise Team to spend time daily in the presence of God in praise and worship, the Word, and in intercession or they would not minister on Sunday. Stop letting people get up in front of people regularly if they are not spending time with God. You are only hurting the people who need to be ministered to and you have someone ministering basically out of his flesh and not by the Spirit of God.

1 Chronicles 16:11 Seek the LORD and his strength, seek his face continually.

Psalms 105:4 Seek the LORD, and his strength: seek his face evermore.

Proverbs 28:5 Evil men understand not judgment: but they that seek the LORD understand all things.

Finally, David returned home to bless his house. *Don't stop there. Maintain your altar at home.* If you are not effectively ministering unto the Lord at home, it will show in ministry, at work, and in your life.

Ps 63:6 When I remember thee upon my bed, and meditate on thee in the night watches.

It is not as hard as one might think in staying in an attitude of praise and worship unto the Lord. Make it a part of your lifestyle. I praise God many days on my way to work. I sing to myself (not all loud so everyone can hear) at my desk, making melody in my heart unto the Lord. Sometimes I get so overjoyed that I have to run to the bathroom. The family car has become our studio. We sing praise and worship songs constantly on trips as we drive. I take time during the day to confess the Word and thank God for His goodness. I just keep a consciousness of Him about me all through the day and night.

The word, "meditate" means *to chew, or to study.* So I would take maybe just one scripture or a principle and think on it, chew on it all day, getting revelation from God. Stop trying to make your time with God a super spiritual thing. He is in you, and living in you. If you call His name, He will answer within.

We have emphasized the "prayer closet" so much that Christians think that they have to go in their special room, lock the door, lay out the blanket, and fall prostrate on their face to God and talk in King James' English. When the Word says "Speaking to yourselves in spiritual songs, hymns, psalms, making melody in your heart unto the Lord" it sounds like a lifestyle to me and not a religious function.

By doing this you won't have to feel guilty come Sunday morning about how much time you spent before God that week. David realized that without due order, there will not be God's due presence. It cost Uzzah his life and David initially lost face with the Jewish leaders.

Nadab and Abihu

These were the sons, of Aaron who made a fatal error in offering unto the Lord "strange fire."

Leviticus 9:22-10:3

22   *And Aaron lifted up his hand toward the people, and blessed them, and came down from offering of the sin offering, and the burnt offering, and peace offerings.*

23   *And Moses and Aaron went into the tabernacle of the congregation, and came out, and blessed the people: and the glory of the LORD appeared unto all the people.*

24   *And there came a fire out from before the LORD, and consumed upon the altar the burnt offering and the fat: which when all the people saw, they shouted, and fell on their faces.*

CHAPTER 10:1-3

1   *And Nadab and Abihu, the sons of Aaron, took either of them his censer, and put fire therein, and put incense thereon, and offered strange fire before the LORD, which he commanded them not.*

2   *And there went out fire from the LORD, and devoured them, and they died before the LORD.*

3   *Then Moses said unto Aaron, This is it that the LORD spake, saying, I will be sanctified in them that come nigh me, and before all the people I will be glorified. And Aaron held his peace.*

Once again, we see the folly in not worshipping God after the due order. Nadab and Abihu were the sons of Aaron, but it was not their time to offer up fire before the Lord.

Exodus 30:6-11

6   *And thou shalt put it before the vail that is by the ark of the testimony, before the mercy seat that is over the testimony, where I will meet with thee.*

7   *And Aaron shall burn thereon sweet incense every morning: when he dresseth the lamps, he shall burn incense upon it.*

8   *And when Aaron lighteth the lamps at even, he shall burn incense upon it, a perpetual incense before the LORD throughout your generations.*

9   *Ye shall offer no strange incense thereon, nor burnt sacrifice, nor meat offering; neither shall ye pour drink offering thereon.*

10   *And Aaron shall make an atonement upon the horns of it once in a year with the blood of the sin offering of atonements: once in the year shall he make atonement upon it throughout your generations: it is most holy unto the LORD.*

The point of their offence is that they lighted the incense at an unauthorized time. God had indeed required the priests to burn incense, but certain priests were tasked to perform the service at different times. Nadab and Abihu did not take direction from Moses. Without receiving orders, or so much as asking leave from him, they took their censers, and they entered into the tabernacle, at the door of which they thought they had attended long enough, and burned incense.

God requires that not only we obey His authority, but also the authority He has established here on earth, most importantly, the church. Moses was their leader. They disobeyed him and took off without his direction. Second, they entered the tabernacle based upon their own self-righteousness rather than God's. ***They thought they had attended that door long enough.*** *Remember that it is not a matter of time, but of timing. When we operate in the will of God, by the Spirit of God, at the time God directs, we will be successful in ministry and successful in life.* God has a time for everything, but it's in His timing.

God had allowed the sons of Aaron to see part of His glory (read **Exodus 24:1-9**). Nadab and Abihu were privileged to accompany Moses, Aaron, and 70 elders of Israel as they ascended Mount Sinai to be near the Lord (**Ex. 24:1-10**). They were consecrated priests, appointed to minister at the tabernacle, so they were on cloud nine, so to speak and felt that they had arrived.

Exodus 24:1 And he said unto Moses, Come up unto the LORD, thou, and Aaron, Nadab, and Abihu, and seventy of the elders of Israel; and worship ye afar off.

The priests also doomed themselves by their blasphemous act. The fire they offered up was also considered to be unholy, based upon the supposition that they were intoxicated (**Leviticus. 10:9**).

The Amplified Bible notes that God was angry not only because of their disobedience, but *because they tried to please God their way and not His way. We need to be entirely surrendered to God's Will and not our own.*

Is God Glorified?

Nadab and Abihu perished before the Lord because of their irreverence towards God and not hallowing the name of the Lord before His people. God will be glorified and honored. He will not share His glory with anyone. When we step out of His will and His direction, we are now on our own course and all of our self-efforts, self-goals, self-indulgences, do nothing to win the favor of God.

The fire, which had previously sanctified the ministry of Aaron as well-pleasing to God, now brought to destruction his two eldest sons because they did not sanctify Yahweh in their hearts, but dared to perform a self-willed act of worship. The same is so in the book of Corinthians where the Gospel of Christ is to one a savor of life unto life and to another a savor of death unto death.

2 Corinthians 2:15,16

15   *For we are unto God a sweet savour of Christ, in them that are saved, and in them that perish:*

16   *To the one we are the savour of death unto death; and to the other the savour of life unto life. And who is sufficient for these things?*

The difference in being a sweet smelling savor unto the Lord or to have the scent of death where no life is produced is based upon our obedience to God and our desire to see Him glorified above all else. Many churches glory in their choir, their band, and even in their piety, but if God is not glorified, then it reeks of the smell of death. Jesus talked about the Pharisees being beautiful sepulchers, but full of dead men bones because they did not glorify God in their hearts and didn't even recognize His Son who stood before them. You see, when you trust in yourself, you lose sight of the Savior. *Self-Efforts without the Spirit is, as far as God is concerned, Effortless.*

Was it a thing of pride that caused them to step out on their own without order and instead of taking of the fire from the altar, which was newly kindled from before the Lord, they took their own fire? God's grace is sufficient to help you and strengthen you, but pride hinders us from receiving from God when we try to do things our own way. *We have to trust in a God who is wise to prescribe His own worship, just to require what he has prescribed, and powerful to revenge what he has not prescribed. (Matthew Henry's Commentary)*

Keeping the Flesh out of our Worship

Ezekiel 44:18
18   *They shall have linen bonnets upon their heads, and shall have linen breeches upon their loins; they shall not gird themselves with any thing that causeth sweat.*

The priests were commanded to wear linen garments when they went in to minister or do any service in the inner court, or in the sanctuary, and nothing that was woolen, because it would cause sweat, v. 17, 18. They were instructed to dress themselves cool, that they might go the more readily about their work; and they had more need to do so because they were to attend the altars, which had constant fires upon them. They also had to dress themselves clean and sweet, and avoid every thing that was sweaty and filthy, to signify the purity of mind with which the service of God is to be attended to. When they had finished their service they had to change their clothes again, and lay up their linen garments in the chambers appointed for that purpose.

God does not like flesh in His presence. **Romans 8:8** says, "*So then they that are in the flesh cannot please God.*" The priests were to wear linen garments to keep themselves cool and from getting too overheated while serving God. This does not mean you can't sweat while worshipping. The analogy used here by the Spirit of God is teaching us to stay in line with the Spirit and avoid acts of the flesh that do not please God. Just as the priests, we are to keep ourselves pure from the outer influences of the world and do not even wear our holy garments around them so to speak. Don't cast your pearls to the swine, aligning yourselves with people who do not worship God out of a pure heart. Once again, consecration and sanctification is stressed.

"Concerning their diet; they must be sure to drink no wine when they went in to minister, lest they should drink to excess, should drink and forget the law, (v. 21)." When we allow ourselves to drink too much from the world, even too much wine, we forget the importance of obeying God. As ministers, we are supposed to be able to teach what is right and wrong and we can't do it all out in the world. God has a divine order that must be obeyed when we come into His presence as a congregation and in our own individual worship. Your lifestyle is a part of your worship to Him, so live circumspectly and soberly as God is glorified not only in your songs, but also in your life.

Moses and the Rock

Numbers 20:8-12

8   *Take the rod, and gather thou the assembly together, thou, and Aaron thy brother, and speak ye unto the rock before their eyes; and it shall give forth his water, and thou shalt bring forth to them water out of the rock: so thou shalt give the congregation and their beasts drink.*

9   *And Moses took the rod from before the LORD, as he commanded him.*

10   *And Moses and Aaron gathered the congregation together before the rock, and he said unto them, Hear now, ye rebels; must we fetch you water out of this rock?*

11   *And Moses lifted up his hand, and with his rod he smote the rock
        twice: and the water came out abundantly, and the congregation
        drank, and their beasts also.*

12   *And the LORD spake unto Moses and Aaron, Because ye believed
        me not, to sanctify me in the eyes of the children of Israel, therefore
        ye shall not bring this congregation into the land.*

Moses did not enter into the Promised Land, because he failed to glorify God by striking the rock twice. ***God told him to speak to the Rock.*** Before this, Moses was told to strike the rock only once. Moses allowed his anger and the people to cheat him out of receiving the promise. When we lash out in the flesh and disobey God, especially before the people, we will not receive the blessings from our service to Him. It doesn't mean that people won't get blessed, but the disobedient servant will lose out. God in the past had told him to strike the rock with the rod, but He did not want the people to put their trust in the rod. This is why He told Moses to speak to the rock, so that they would recognize the power of the Word of God. This Word, who would soon come in the form of Jesus.

Praise and Worship in God's due order is a matter of faith. We act in faith, believing that God will respond if we call out to Him out of a pure heart. We believe that as we intercede, praise, and worship Him, He will make His abode with us and with Him come all the provisions we need to grow and develop spiritually, mentally, emotionally, physically, financially, and socially. Your faith and trust must be in Him and not your praise band, church, or in your own self-righteousness. God has placed those in the church to assist you in your worship to Him, but they cannot substitute for Him.

JEREMIAH 2:13: "For my people have committed two sins: They have forsaken me, the spring of living water, and have dug their own cisterns, broken cisterns that cannot hold water." (NIV)

Moses had begun to think that he was the source and not God. In the above scripture, many times, we dig our own wells and look to other sources other than God. It's interesting that God considers it a sin when we forsake Him. In the desert, there were springs of water that ran from various tributaries, so there would be an abundant supply of water to refresh and satisfy your thirst. However, many of the Israelites were foolish enough to go and try to dig their own wells. These wells were not linked to any other sources, so they would have water one day, but on the return trip, they may find the well dried up.

Can you worship God without your choir? Do you have to put in a tape in order to have a praise service in your personal time? Are you able to serve God without all the trappings provided to you by the church? If the answer is no, then you have created broken cisterns that can hold no water. To many Christians, social fellowships, their music boxes, and bible meetings, is their time with God. They cannot spend a minute in the presence of God on their own. All of these things are good, but they cannot substitute for your time alone with the Father.

God was speaking of the living water as the Spirit. Jesus spoke of the Holy Spirit as *"Living Waters."* If we believe in God, then rivers of living waters will flow in us, replenishing and nourishing us, and then out through us to minister to others. So stop looking for substitutes when you can have the real thing. Don't trust in the staff, but in the Word of God. All Moses had to do was to speak to the Rock and the needs of the people would have been fulfilled without him paying the cost of disobedience. God's anger kindled against Moses because he failed to glorify Him and His Word in the midst of the congregation.

God establishes a divine order so that He will be glorified and His people edified, prospered, blessed, strengthened and empowered to do His work in the earth. When we deviate from His divine order, then we lose out on what He has for us.

Doing it the way He commanded

2 Chronicles 5:11-6:1

11   And it came to pass, when the priests were come out of the holy place: (for all the priests that were present were sanctified, and did not then wait by course:

12   Also the Levites which were the singers, all of them of Asaph, of Heman, of Jeduthun, with their sons and their brethren, being arrayed in white linen, having cymbals and psalteries and harps, stood at the east end of the altar, and with them an hundred and twenty priests sounding with trumpets:)

13   It came even to pass, as the trumpeters and singers were as one, to make one sound to be heard in praising and thanking the LORD; and when they lifted up their voice with the trumpets and cymbals and instruments of musick, and praised the LORD, saying, For he is good; for his mercy endureth for ever: that then the house was filled with a cloud, even the house of the LORD;

14   So that the priests could not stand to minister by reason of the cloud: for the glory of the LORD had filled the house of God.

It should be the desire of every church to experience the Shekinah presence of the Lord. Here in **2Chronicles 5th chapter**, the glory of the Lord was so strong and so filled the room that the priests could hardly stand to minister. It means they were incapacitated. God took over the service. Wouldn't it be great if God just takes over the service? I mean, to have Him minister unto others and not ever a word spoken or preached.

I've seen this happen before. Once, when our praise team ministered at a nursing home, we began to sing this song about Love. As we sang, the power of God came on the scene. It was so strong and so tangible that it seemed like no one could move or knew what to say. Then all of a sudden, people started getting out of their wheel chairs. One man came up to me and I placed my hand over his right eye and he received his sight again in that eye. I placed my fingers in one man's ears and he received his hearing. There were people who said that had not walked in years, were able to move again. It was powerful! We were all amazed at what God was doing in that place.

Many people desire to see the "glory cloud," but it doesn't come easy. To experience God's presence in a greater manifestation as in 2 Chronicles 5th chapter, four things must take place: **Consecration, Preparation, Dedication, and Unification.**

<u>Consecration</u>. The word, consecration is used synonymous with sanctification meaning to be set apart for service. The priests had to be first consecrated unto the service of the Lord. This requires living a life that is holy and committed to God. As we come to the Father, to be used of Him, we need to keep our lives set apart unto Him. **2 Timothy 2:3 says, "No one engaged in warfare entangles himself with the affairs of this life, that he may please him who enlisted him as a soldier."** (NIV) A soldier engaged in military service is initially separated from civilian life so that he won't be distracted from his duty to his/her country. God wants pure, holy, and committed vehicles so that He can use for His glory. The priests had to be first consecrated before they could attend the service.

They came out of the Holy Place. They had to be cleansed before they could minister unto others. Many times we forget this in our churches. We have people who are talented and desiring to be used, but still have problems with sin in their lives. We all have problems with sin, but if it becomes too habitual and without remorse, then this person needs to be removed from the eyes of others. He or she is too distracted with sin and the things of this world to be involved in service. The Levites came out of the holy place into the place to lead others in worship.

Without Keeping their Divisions. The Levites were divided into 24 groups of priests, chosen to assist in general temple responsibilities. However, as the scripture states, *"They did not then wait by course."* Members from all the twenty-four courses assisted on this important occasion. The normal rotations in service could come later! All who are involved in ministry must be consecrated and separated unto the Lord, regardless of your responsibility, status, or calling. Also, all members of the congregation, no matter what your position or status may be, must be involved in praise and worship. Too many times, worship is going on and you may see the ushers, deacons, or even ministers talking and carrying on during the service. This shows irreverence for the presence of God and it hinders God from moving in the service. Everyone should be involved in praise and worship. Before we can be an effective minister before others, we must take time to minister in His presence.

Preparation. The second element in seeing the presence of God manifested in your life and in your church is to prepare yourself physically, spiritually, and emotionally for the service of the Lord. In **2 Timothy 2:5**, Paul compares the Christian walk to that of an athlete: **"And also if anyone competes in athletics, he is not crowned unless he competes according to the rules."** An athlete must train himself diligently in order to gain the prize. **1 Corinthians 9:27** says, that he must buffet or discipline his body in order to run effectively. A disciple is a "disciplined follower." He or she is a person who is willing to train himself/herself spiritually and emotionally in order to perform the service he/she has been called to.

You must compete according to the rules. The task of Preparation must be in line with the Word of God, or you will forfeit the prize. Many musicians and singers prepare themselves physically and musically for their task, but do little spiritually. In my early years as a minister of music, it was required that we come to 5:00 a.m. prayer meetings and bible study before we could sing. Our praise practice, sometimes, consisted of an hour of singing in the spirit or praying before we worked on the mechanics of the song. We put the ministry of the Lord first to ensure that the anointing and presence of God was strong in us before we considered all the workings involved in performing the song. *We practiced the presence of God.* In other words, we prepared ourselves to be accustomed to God's presence so that when we ministered, we were able to hear His voice, and obey His Word.

There are sometimes in the service God, you may want to minister a Word of Knowledge or operate in the gifts of the Spirit. If you are not accustomed to His voice, you will just continue on singing without any ministering. People may get excited and happy, but afterwards, they are empty again. We were taught that we are doing a disservice to others and evil before God if we did not prepare our hearts to seek God's face.

"And he did evil, because he did not prepare his heart to seek the Lord."

King Rehoboam of Jerusalem (the southern part of Judah) refused to diligently seek and inquire of the Lord. Because of this, he experienced only wars, and troubles, eventually dying without any recognition of his accomplishments as king. He started out good and God helped him establish his kingdom, but he later forsook the Lord and all Israel along with him. You see, when a person in authority falls, it affects the whole body. That is why as a person leading the people in praise, your lifestyle, your commitment, and your service is crucial to those who look to you to lead them into the presence of God. Guard your heart (your spirit), and guard the word in your heart. Prepare yourself by seeking His face and strengthening yourself to perform the service of the Lord. Don't carry all your problems, burdens, strife, and such when you stand before others. Strip yourself as much as possible as you minister. **Proper Preparation Promotes Powerful Performances.**

<u>**DEDICATION.**</u> We must be dedicated to the task. In **2 Timothy 2:6,** Paul now refers to the farmer as hardworking and dedicated to the field he tends in order to make a living. There is no one more dedicated than the farmer, who may have to wait for months before seeing the fruit of his labor. *"The hardworking farmer must be first to partake of the crops."* Each scripture in **2 Timothy 2:4-6** talks about a reward or recognition that is received when a person properly consecrates himself

to service, prepares himself, and dedicates himself to the task. There is a song that says, "Nothing from nothing leaves nothing and you gotta have something if you want to deal with me." If you apply nothing then you will receive nothing. Many people want something, but they can't be counted upon to do something. They become frustrated in ignorance wondering why nothing is happening in their lives.

God is a rewarder of them that diligently seek Him (**Hebrews 11:6**). We are to dedicate ourselves to the task of seeking His face, spending time in His presence. The reward of the people involved in the worship that day was the presence of God and to experience His glory. You can't get anything better than that.

UNIFICATION. The Bible says in **2 Chronicles 5:13** that they became as one to make one sound in praise unto the Lord. ***Unity in praise is the pathway to God's presence.*** God is not the author of confusion, but of peace and love (**1 Corinthians 14:33**). When His people become of one mind, one spirit, united in praise and united in purpose, He responds with His presence. **Psalms 133:1** reveals to us that when God's people come together in unity, the anointing is released. That is why it is so important to lay aside differences, strife, envy, and every evil work, when we come together as a church. We are encouraged only to bring a psalm, a hymn, or a spiritual song that we might exhort and comfort one another. The Word of God constantly reminds us to be of one mind, speaking the same thing (**Romans 12:16**), endeavoring to keep the unity of the faith in the bond of peace (**Ephesians 4:3**).

It is the responsibility of every believer to pursue unity. That is why God hates those who sow discord and cause strife among others (Proverbs 6:16-19). It hinders His ability to minister to His people. We are to become as one with the Father and with one another.

The glory of the Lord that had filled the temple, some say, was reference to the Holy Spirit. Psalms 133:1 talks about the anointing that is released when people dwell in unity. The disciples were in one accord when they received the Holy Spirit in **Act 2:1**. Need I say more? To be in *"one accord"* means to be unanimous, being in agreement, having one mind and purpose. The body of Christ must be in volitional agreement in order to experience in greater dimensions, the power of God's presence.

Many times as a worship leader, I would exhort the congregation to lift their hands unto the Lord. There are always a few that would not specifically because they were asked to. They think they are proving to themselves and others that they are above instruction, but all they are doing is being a hindrance to the body. Thank God many times He overlooks them and ministers to His people. However, those who rebel are the ones who are losing out.

God wants to be a blessing to His people and rain down His presence so that we may be refreshed, strengthen, healed, encouraged, blessed, and saved. He provided instruction in His Word and has given us the Holy Spirit so that we might be able to establish our relationship with Him and come to know the pathway to His throne room. There is a prescribed order for achieving this as David and Solomon learned. Those who fail to obey God's Word and step out on their own may reap disastrous results as in the case with Uzzah, Abihu, and Nadab. Moses failed to enter the Promised Land because of it, and today, many believers fail to receive the promises of God and experience the beauty of the Lord. I encourage you today, to incorporate these teachings in your life, so that you can experience more of God.

Chapter Eight

▼

Victory In Praise

I experienced the greatest victories in my life when I "praise through." In other words, I have seen the hand of God move strong in my life when I allowed praise to go before me. There is victory in praise. Praise can shake up the very foundations of your life, and as others see it demonstrated through you and in you, they in turn glorify God and come to know the power of your God. Paul and Silas in Acts, the 16th chapter, unleashed God's power in a mighty way by not looking at their circumstances, but looking unto the Father, praising His name aloud and with joy.

Acts 16:22-31
22   *And the multitude rose up together against them: and the magistrates rent off their clothes, and commanded to beat them.*
23   *And when they had laid many stripes upon them, they cast them into prison, charging the jailor to keep them safely:*
24   *Who, having received such a charge, thrust them into the inner prison, and made their feet fast in the stocks.*

25 *And at midnight Paul and Silas prayed, and sang praises unto God: and the prisoners heard them.*

26 *And suddenly there was a great earthquake, so that the foundations of the prison were shaken: and immediately all the doors were opened, and every one's bands were loosed.*

27 *And the keeper of the prison awaking out of his sleep, and seeing the prison doors open, he drew out his sword, and would have killed himself, supposing that the prisoners had been fled.*

28 *But Paul cried with a loud voice, saying, Do thyself no harm: for we are all here.*

29 *Then he called for a light, and sprang in, and came trembling, and fell down before Paul and Silas,*

30 *And brought them out, and said, Sirs, what must I do to be saved?*

31 *And they said, Believe on the Lord Jesus Christ, and thou shalt be saved, and thy house.*

Praise and Worship unleashes the power of God to give you the victory over your circumstances, your flesh, and over the trials in your life. We must learn to minister unto the Lord, before, during, and after we receive the victory in our life. We need to keep praising Him afterwards, maintaining a life style of praise for the "Avenger" (Psalms 8:2) cometh quickly to take what you have received.

Exodus 15:19-21

19 *For the horse of Pharaoh went in with his chariots and with his horsemen into the sea, and the LORD brought again the waters of the sea upon them; but the children of Israel went on dry land in the midst of the sea.*

20 *And Miriam the prophetess, the sister of Aaron, took a timbrel in her hand; and all the women went out after her with timbrels and with dances.*

21   *And Miriam answered them, Sing ye to the LORD, for he hath triumphed gloriously; the horse and his rider hath he thrown into the sea.*

Remember we discussed that Moses knew God ways (Psalms 103:7). Moses knew what God was able and willing to do. He stood on God's Word knowing that God would deliver them and give them the victory. You see, it requires Faith to praise the Father and in the interim (in the midst of our praise to Him), He stimulates our faith so that we can wait on Him and see the salvation or the victory of the Lord.

Exodus 14:10-14

10   *And when Pharaoh drew nigh, the children of Israel lifted up their eyes, and, behold, the Egyptians marched after them; and they were sore afraid: and the children of Israel cried out unto the LORD.*

11   *And they said unto Moses, Because there were no graves in Egypt, hast thou taken us away to die in the wilderness? wherefore hast thou dealt thus with us, to carry us forth out of Egypt?*

12   *Is not this the word that we did tell thee in Egypt, saying, Let us alone, that we may serve the Egyptians? For it had been better for us to serve the Egyptians, than that we should die in the wilderness.*

13   *And Moses said unto the people, Fear ye not, stand still, and see the salvation of the LORD, which he will shew to you to day: for the Egyptians whom ye have seen to day, ye shall see them again no more for ever.*

14   *The LORD shall fight for you, and ye shall hold your peace.*

God wants to show you His saving power over your situations. Moses exhorted the people to "Stand still." This means to stop trying to bring it to pass by your own means or activities. Sometimes, we just have to "Let Go and Let God." Through Praise, we release the situation unto the Lord, and He composes our minds, and strengthens our heart that we may be able to stand in the midst of turbulence and not take flight. Too many times, when trouble comes, we immediately want to run or to evade the situation. We may run to the arm of flesh, when God just wants us *to be still* in His presence and allow Him to work on our behalf.

Moses directs the children of Israel to leave it to God. Do not take flight or fight. Take time to hear from God and receive His orders. It is in His presence that we receive guidance and instructions on how to win in the midst of adversity. We also await God's presence so that we may be strengthened and encouraged to keep standing. We compose ourselves, by an entire confidence in God, into a peaceful prospect of the great salvation God is now about to work for us.

Another man who knew how important it was to stand and wait was Jehoshaphat. When surrounded by two enemies, all Jehoshaphat could say, *"Lord, I do not know what to do, but my eyes are upon you."(2 Chronicles 20:12)* Instead of cowering in fear, he responded by setting his face to seek the Lord. That's when he received God's instruction for the kingdom to praise Him before the battle and stand and see how He would give them the victory.

God spoke to them saying, *"Position yourselves, stand still, and see the salvation of the Lord, who is with you."(2 Chronicles 20:17) When you respond to the Lord in praise, giving Him thanks in advance for what He is able and about to do, God positions you in a place where you can see the move of His mighty hand.* Jehoshaphat and his people bowed and worshipped the Lord and praised Him with loud voices on high. They trusted in His words and responded in praise and worship. The very next day, they stepped out in faith, having people appointed to go forth in praise, before the army! Then they positioned themselves to see the enemy defeated before them. There comes a time when mortal resources will not help you. When your back is against the wall, Look up! Position yourself in prayer, praise, and worship, and wait for God's mighty arm to bring salvation, deliverance, power, and blessings.

We serve a victorious God, so we praise Him always for the victory (**Psalms 98:1**).

Psalms 98:1 Oh sing to the Lord a new song! For He has done marvelous things; His right hand and His holy arm have gained Him the victory. (NIV)

The Amplified adds to this by saying, *"his Holy arm have wrought salvation for Him."* There is a song that the angels cannot sing and it is the song of redemption. The blood of the Lamb has redeemed us and He has won for us the victory! Therefore, we praise Him for His mighty acts and excellent greatness. Those high praises of God in our mouths should be of victory and not defeat. Shout unto the Lord with a voice of triumph!

Psalms 47:1: O clap your hands, all ye people; shout unto God with the voice of triumph.

This psalm is a triumphal ode, and was probably composed to be sung on occasion of some military triumph. If God has given us the victory or if we expect in faith that He will give us the victory, our immediate response is Praise. The Jews celebrated with a solemn procession on a return from battle, with captive princes marching in the procession, and with a display of the "shields" and other implements of war taken from the foe. Songs were sung to Thank God for His intervening power, bringing them the victory. God reveals once again His purpose to protect his chosen people in time of peril.

We express our victory by "clapping our hands." This is a common way of expressing joy. We applaud others for their efforts or in response to someone who is worthy of honor. Isn't this just like our God who is mighty and worthy to receive our praise and honor?

Another expression is "shouting." We shout or make a joyful noise in praise of God in acknowledgment that this victory has been gained by His intervention and not by our works. For it is not by might, nor by power, but by my Spirit says the Lord (**Zechariah 4:6**). We shout with a voice of triumph in faith expecting positive results. There are doubtless times when loud shouts, as expressions of joy, are proper. Jehoshaphat and all of Judah responded with loud shouts unto the Lord. Sometimes, you have to shout above the voice of the devil. He is throwing his darts and trying to bring thoughts of fear and doubt. So I shout that I can't hear him. It really works.

2 Corinthians 2:14 Now thanks be unto God, which always causeth us to triumph in Christ, and maketh manifest the savour of his knowledge by us in every place.

A believer's triumphs are all in Christ. In ourselves we are weak, and have neither joy nor victory; but in Christ we may rejoice and triumph. True believers have constant cause of triumph in Christ, for they are more than conquerors through him who hath loved them (**Romans. 8:37**). Because God has given us the victory, He has given us reason to rejoice. The good news of the gospel is a good reason for a Christian's joy and rejoicing.

CHAPTER NINE

▼

PRAISE AND THE ANOINTING

Praise is directly linked to the anointing in the life of the believer. Praise releases the anointing of God on the scene. It helps us to maintain the anointing in our life. Finally, it keeps us in harmony with the Holy Spirit.

Psalms 133:1-2
1   *Behold, how good and how pleasant it is for brethren to dwell together in unity!*
2   *It is like the precious ointment upon the head, that ran down upon the beard, even Aaron's beard: that went down to the skirts of his garments;*

The anointing spoken of in the above scripture speaks of an anointing that occurs physically with a substance such as oil, myrrh, or balsam. But this is also a spiritual anointing, as the Holy Spirit anoints a person's heart and mind with the love and truth of God. It also teaches us the things that God has prepared for us.

What is the anointing? What does it mean to anoint? Well the word, "anoint" means to authorize, or set apart for a particular work or service (**Isaiah 61:1; Luke 4:18**). I also like to think of the anointing as God's presence. *The Anointing represents God's presence, God's virtue, and God's power.* We are separated as believers from the world because we have the presence of God abiding on the inside of us. We are empowered by Him, and His nature becomes our nature.

Isaiah 43:21 says how God fashioned and formed a people for Himself to render or demonstrate praise. We are called God's anointed, being sealed with a special seal and adopted into the Family of God. He filled us with His spirit so that we could minister more effectively unto Him. The Holy Spirit guides us and directs us in our worship unto the Father.

How is the Anointing Released?

Praise releases the anointing. When God's people come together in unity and render praise unto Him, the anointing is released. We read how when the singers and trumpeters became as one in making one sound to be heard in praising God, and how God's glory came and that the priests could hardly stand to minister because of God's glory (2 Chronicles 5:11-15).

Faith releases the anointing. We must go to the Lord in expectancy, believing that God is more than able. Janny Grein once said in her book, **Called, Appointed, and Anointed**, *"You must believe (know) that you are anointed by God, and to trust, lean, and depend upon that anointing."* [1] **1 John 2:27** says, we have received an anointing (unction) from the Holy One.[1] God has anointed you, and that anointing is enhanced when you know that you know that you know that you are anointed.

---

[1]   Janny Grein. <u>Called, Appointed, Anointed.</u> Tulsa Books. 1964

Unity releases the anointing. Within the church, it is body of Christ becoming as one that releases the presence of God. A church riddled with division, strife, contentions, and envy, will not experience the power of God. The key to success of the New Testament Church was through their unity.

We Increase in the Anointing by Desiring God's Presence

Psalms 27:4-6

4   *One thing have I desired of the LORD, that will I seek after; that I may dwell in the house of the LORD all the days of my life, to behold the beauty of the LORD, and to inquire in his temple.*

5   *For in the time of trouble he shall hide me in his pavilion: in the secret of his tabernacle shall he hide me; he shall set me up upon a rock.*

6   *And now shall mine head be lifted up above mine enemies round about me: therefore will I offer in his tabernacle sacrifices of joy; I will sing, yea, I will sing praises unto the LORD.*

David longed for the presence of God. His desire was to dwell in His house and to behold His beauty. He knew that in His presence was fullness of joy, power, strength, wisdom, and knowledge. God's anointing empowers us to go forth and do what He called us to do. As we spend time in God's presence, God's unction, His anointing, ministers unto us, teaches us all things, and strengthens us in our walk, our ministry, our household, and our work. Mary knew that if she spent time at Jesus' feet, her work would be more fruitful. The early church incorporated the anointing in their work, by spending time with the Father.

Acts 4:13 Now when they saw the boldness of Peter and John, and perceived that they were unlearned and ignorant men, they marvelled; and they took knowledge of them, that they had been with Jesus.

The people witnessed and experienced the power of God through Peter and John. They marveled and took notice that they had been with Jesus. When you are in the presence of God, it is revealed in the presence of others. The key to success in ministry, life, home, is spending time with the Father.

Why Do We Need the Anointing in Our Lives?

Luke 4:18 "The Spirit of the Lord is upon me, because he hath anointed me to preach the gospel to the poor; he hath sent me to heal the brokenhearted, to preach deliverance to the captives, and recovering of sight to the blind, to set at liberty them that are bruised,"

As believers, we need the anointing in our lives. Remember, When Paul and Silas praised God, and the prisoners heard them. They were set free when God sent an earthquake to the prison and everyone bonds were loose. As we praise the Father, we are strengthened by Him to do the works He has called us to do. It is the anointing that breaks the yoke of bondage over people lives. Jesus was anointed to preach the gospel to those held captive by the enemy (the devil), to heal the brokenhearted, to set at liberty though who are bruised (defeated, hurt), and recovery of sight to the blind. He was empowered to do this by the Spirit of God operating in His life. He was anointed and empowered by the Holy Spirit.

Isaiah 10:27 And it shall come to pass in that day, that his burden shall be taken away from off thy shoulder, and his yoke from off thy neck, and the yoke shall be destroyed because of the anointing.

We are empowered by God's Spirit to do the works of Jesus. We are more effective if we live a life of praise and worship, walking in communion with the Father. Where are you drawing your strength today? Are you seeking the Lord with all your heart, allowing Him to cover you with the ointment of His spirit? The yoke of bondage, fear, distress, can be broken over your life and the lives of others as you and I incorporate the anointing of God in our life through praise and worship.

Final Encouragement

I encourage you today to make praise a way of life. *As praise goes before you, God goes before you, and will give you the victory.* There is power in praise and as I said earlier, **Proper Preparation (according to God's divine order) Promotes Powerful Performances by God, in your church, and in your life.** There is no greater weapon for the believer today as when he learns to incorporate praise in his lifestyle. Through worship and praise, we can gain a greater and more intimate knowledge of our Father and establish our relationship with Him, so that our faith is renewed and strengthened. We can experience the victory from His mighty acts, yet come to know His ways and His heart.

I hope that this book has helped you to gain an understanding of what is available to you as you experience the joy, the power, the influence, and the blessings of praise. You are a king and a priest, God's chosen vessel, created by God for the purpose of demonstrating His praise in the earth. Go forth and show the world what a mighty God we serve and encourage them to praise Him to.

LET PRAISE GO BEFORE THEE!

ABOUT THE AUTHOR

Kenneth W. Jones has distinguished himself as a praise leader, psalmist, and now a teacher of the Word of God. His experience includes over 20 years as a minister of music in various churches where he has taught praise and worship to Christians of various faiths and walks of life. After receiving a deeper calling into the five-fold ministry as a teacher of the Gospel, Kenneth has taught in churches all over the world. Currently an officer in the United States Army, God has opened doors for Kenneth to preach in areas such as the Middle East and Europe. Sometimes, he considers himself a Military supported Missionary.

As a minister of the gospel, Kenneth enjoys teaching the principles of Praise and Worship. He desires that churches and the individual believer would come to know the true power and beauty that is available to them through a deeper, intimate, relationship with the Father that is enhanced through praise and worship. He also is the founder of a home-established ministry, *"Practical Living Ministry (PLM)."* PLM's vision is teaching practical concepts for Christian living. He and his lovely wife, Mary publishes a monthly newsletter, *"Laying it on the Vine,"* that encourages and exhorts friends of the ministry in their walk with Christ.

Kenneth and Mary's children include Chasity, Chloe, Kenneth Jr., Enuolare, and recently born twins, Jared and Josiah. As they come to end of their military career, their future vision is to teach God's principles as doors are open. If you would like Kenneth and Mary to speak at your church or more copies of this book, please write us at 158 Greenland Drive, McDonough, Georgia 30253.

0-595-25954-5